SpringerBriefs in Economics

For further volumes:
http://www.springer.com/series/8876

Ad J. W. van de Gevel · Charles N. Noussair

The Nexus Between Artificial Intelligence and Economics

Springer

Ad J. W. van de Gevel
Charles N. Noussair
Department of Economics
Tilburg University
Tilburg, The Netherlands

ISSN 2191-5504 ISSN 2191-5512 (electronic)
ISBN 978-3-642-33647-8 ISBN 978-3-642-33648-5 (eBook)
DOI 10.1007/978-3-642-33648-5
Springer Heidelberg New York Dordrecht London

Library of Congress Control Number: 2012955406

Printed on acid-free paper

Springer is part of Springer Science+Business Media (www.springer.com)

Dedicated to Miriam Thomas Noussair

Contents

The Nexus Between Artificial Intelligence and Economics

Abstract We review recent developments in artificial intelligence and relate them to economics. Artificial intelligence represents the technology most likely to lead to a singularity, an infinite rate of innovation and productivity growth. This could occur via dramatic increases in life expectancy, the development of whole brain emulation, and innovations in robotics. We argue that there is no reason to believe that artificial intelligence would increase human happiness. We describe some recent development in agent-based modeling in economics, which can be interpreted as the introduction of artificially intelligent agents into economics. We argue that classical economic theory, which assumes that all agents are rational and have infinite computational ability, is very relevant in describing the behavior of future artificially intelligent entities. Economic implications of accelerating innovation, greater longevity, and the introduction of robot labor are considered.

Keywords Artificial intelligence • Robotics • Artificial economics • Logistic growth • Singularity • Artificial happiness • Methuselarity • Artificial consciousness • Artificial life • Whole brain emulation

1 Introduction

The history of a science has been described in terms of transitions between paradigms (Kuhn 1962). A paradigm is a set of rules, standards and practices shared by groups of scientists, representing the continuation of a research tradition. For example, nanotechnology has been regarded as a revolutionary technology that is bringing about a paradigm shift in industrial research. Within a particular scientific discipline there are typically periods of stability, or normal science, punctuated by periods of crisis, leading to a revolution and a new normal science. During a stable period, puzzle-solving activities take place in response to a mismatch between the paradigm and reality. The puzzles that cannot be solved are seen as anomalies of a

Ad J. W. van de Gevel and Charles N. Noussair, *The Nexus Between Artificial Intelligence and Economics*, SpringerBriefs in Economics, DOI: 10.1007/978-3-642-33648-5_1, paradigm, which produce disorder or crisis, and which encourage the willingness to try new approaches. The existence of unsolvable puzzles, such as how to overcome the limits of Moore's Law and to benefit from nanotechnology, serves as an incentive to develop a new paradigm.

In this book, we argue that the emergence and development of Artificial Intelligence (AI) represents a paradigm shift in science. While all prior paradigms have been based on an entirely human civilization, AI will create a human–machine civilization. It is likely that during this century the accelerating growth of computer power will result in machine intelligence exceeding human intelligence in capability. AI will outperform the biological portion of humanity. It is even possible that reverse engineering of our software (our minds) and upgrading our hardware (our bodies) may indefinitely extend human life before the dawn of the 22nd century. Humankind will coexist and may ultimately merge with its computational technology. The intelligent beings that would emerge would represent the next stage in evolution. In a few decades, the average human brain may host billions of blood-cell-sized computers that will effectively multiply our biological intelligence a billion fold. This vast inter-neuronal network of computers would allow humans to think at electronic speeds, store worlds of information, and disseminate that information to each other or to all humans instantly.

This book is organized as follows. Section 2 introduces the notion of the Singularity, a stage in development in which technological progress and economic growth increase at a near-infinite rate. Section 3 describes what artificial intelligence is and how it has been applied. Section 4 considers artificial happiness and the likelihood that artificial intelligence might increase human happiness. Section 5 discusses some prominent related concepts and issues. Section 6 describes the use of artificial agents in economic modeling, and Section 7 considers some ways in which economic analysis can offer some hints about what the advent of artificial intelligence might bring. Section 8 presents some thoughts about the current state of AI and its future prospects.

2 Technological Progress: Logistic Growth or Singularity?

Human history has always been characterized by technological advances. One view about the trajectory of technological progress is that it follows a series of logistic processes. According to this view, technological progress develops in three stages: slow growth at first, followed by rapid growth and finally a leveling off, as illustrated by S-shaped curves. Cowan (2011) argues that human civilization is currently on a flat portion of this curve. The advent of artificial intelligence has the promise to alter this pattern. Futurist Kurzweil (2005) asserts that a serious assessment of the history of technology shows that technological change is exponential. In his view the power of future technology is generally underestimated because it is based on a linear extrapolation. For a brief period of time exponential trends appear to be linear, particularly in the early stage of progress. According to

Kurzweil, smarter computers and their integration with human brains will lead to a time when change is so fast and significant that the progress-curve becomes nearly vertical, and technology appears to be improving at infinite speed. This situation has been termed the *Singularity*.

The Singularity is a time of Transhumanism, at which there will be no clear distinction between humans and machines or between physical and virtual reality. Based on recent progress in the fields of neurobiology and nanotechnology, Kurzweil predicts significant steps in the fight against disease and aging, as well as in the augmentation of the human mind. In his opinion, in the future the line between biology and technology will blur and eventually become irrelevant. Humanity would be aided by the interaction with technology and potential pitfalls mitigated by smart technological solutions. Most Singularitarians believe that the Singularity will take place in this century, likely even within several decades. Kurzweil mentions 2045, but other futurists use a more conservative timeframe: 2140.

The most likely cause of the Singularity will be the creation of some form of rapidly *self-enhancing* greater-than-human intelligence. Human intellectual skills have developed thus far through evolution. Our brains today are relatively fixed in design and capacity. Biological human thinking is limited to 1016 calculations per second per human brain. Currently we cannot increase our own brainpower within our lifetimes; in fact we gradually lose neurons as we age. All thought is taking place on neurons with a limiting speed of 200 operations per second with a top speed of the electrochemical signals of 150 m per second along the fastest neurons.

By comparison, the speed of light is 300,000,000 m per second, two million times greater. Speeds in modern computer chips are currently at around 2 GHz, a ten million fold difference over humans and increasing exponentially. Within a few decades computers will have computational power and intelligence vastly greater than the human brain, and non-biological intelligence will be one billion times more powerful than all human intelligence today. The Singularity would result from many intertwined technological revolutions, including in Genetics, Nanotechnology and Robotics (GNR). At this moment the early stages of the *G-revolution* appear to be occurring. The genetic revolution is currently focused on correcting obvious biological flaws. The precise biochemical pathways that underlie both disease and aging processes are being discovered. Scientists are on the verge of being able to control how genes express themselves. This revolution has the promise to greatly increase human longevity, as humans move away from their biological bodies toward a software-based existence.

The *N-revolution* may eventually enable a redesign and rebuilding of human bodies and brains, and indeed the world, molecule by molecule from the bottom up, going beyond the limitations of biology. However, as revolutionary as nanotechnology will be, artificial intelligence will have far more profound consequences, since nanotechnology is powerful but not necessarily intelligent. The most powerful revolution is the *robotic* or *R-revolution*: human-level robots with their artificial computer thinking ability will far exceed human capabilities. This is already well underway, as we discuss in Section 5.5 of the book.

2.1 Empirical Evidence in Favor of the Singularity

Maddison (2008) and Jones (2009) present evidence that per-capita GDP and population growth have been accelerating. Jones, referring to Nordhaus (1997), who links accelerating growth to ideas in his famous "price of light" calculation, postulates that new ideas are at the heart of accelerating population and productivity growth. More people lead to more ideas and more ideas made it possible for the world to support more people. Since population is a power function of the number of ideas, population growth accelerates similarly over time. Hence, both ideas and population would become infinite in a finite period of time if there were no resource constraints. However, since it is biologically impossible for the population growth rate to become infinite, fertility and population growth would eventually level out.

Although demographic projections predict that the number of humans on earth will reach a maximum in this century, which might lead to a slowing of growth in technology, many factors may offset such a slowdown. More intense integration and communication among people allows individuals to share ideas and this factor may continue to grow long after total population begins to decline. Moreover, rising levels of human capital per capita will make the average individual better at discovering and sharing ideas. This effect may be increased if new institutions change incentives.

Market signals point to acceleration in the rate of innovation in recent decades. There is a trend toward shorter corporate longevity. In the 1950s the average turnover in the S&P 500, measured by additions and deletions to the index, was about 3–4 % per annum, suggesting an average life, as a component of the index, of about 25–35 years. The current annual turnover in the S&P 500 is about 7–8 %, corresponding to an average company life just 12–14 years. The weighting of technology companies in the stock market is four times greater than it was a decade ago at 28 vs. 7 % (Mauboussin and Schay 2000).

Furthermore, individual company share price volatility is increasing (Campbell et al. 2001). While the market's overall volatility is currently well within historical bounds, the volatility of individual stocks has been increasing sharply since the early 1960s, revealing greater turnover in individual company prospects.

The global economy is moving from physical to knowledge assets. This increases the stakes of success and failure. Evidence of this transition is provided by the sharp increase in Tobin's q ratio, the ratio between market price and balance sheet asset value. One calculation shows that the q ratio rose from about 0.5 in 1980 to 2.5 in 2000 (Mauboussin and Schay 2000). In many knowledge sectors firms compete in winner-take-all or winner-take-most markets in which the strong get stronger and the weak get weaker. Examples of winners include Microsoft (PC operating systems), Google (online search engines) and eBay (consumer online auctions). Shareholder returns for the top firms are increasing, while the declines for the losers are getting steeper.

2.2 *Living Forever: Methuselarity*

A great deal of human effort goes into avoiding and delaying death. Aubrey de Grey (2008) has suggested that a succession of advances in age reduction will surpass a critical threshold, which he terms *Methuselarity*. Methuselarity is the bio-gerontological counterpart of the Singularity. Methuselarity is the point at which people can expect to live, without age-related physiological and cognitive decline, from a low-three-digit to an infinite number of years. Aging will be subject to comprehensive postponement by regenerative medicine which partially or completely restores a damaged biological structure to its pre-damaged state. When rejuvenation therapies are sufficient to deplete the damage from aging more rapidly than it is accumulating, Methuselarity (longevity escape velocity) will have been reached.

According to de Grey, the transition to Methuselarity will take no longer than a few years to arrive. Although he predicts a progressive, smooth, modest, relatively slow and unbroken decline in the rate at which new anti-aging therapies will be developed once LEV is first achieved, only quite *modest rates of progress* will be sufficient to greatly postpone aging. Ultra-powerful computers would assist in attaining these innovations. De Grey predicts that the first thousand-year-old human is probably less than 20 years younger than the first 150-year-old. The first million-year-old and billion-year-old are probably less than a year younger than the first thousand-year-old.

2.3 *The Avatar Roadmap to Human Immortality*

Russian media magnate Dmitry Itskov is heading "Avatar," an extraordinarily ambitious and far-reaching multidisciplinary research project that aims to achieve immortality in humans within the next three decades (Borghino 2012). He plans to do it by housing human brains in progressively more disembodied vehicles, first transplanting them into robots and then, by the year 2045, reverse-engineering the human brain and effectively "downloading" human consciousness onto a computer chip.

Speculating on seemingly unachievable goals like this one is subject to a cognitive trap, the belief that improbable technological advances automatically become more likely simply by looking further away in the future. Itskov's project seems to suffer from this trap. The principle of the late professor in astronomy Carl Sagan, which states that "extraordinary claims demand extraordinary evidence," seems to apply here. However, with the rate of technological change continuing to accelerate, the Avatar's goals may be within reach, but not necessarily within the project's aggressive timeline.

The first of the proposed steps, to be completed before 2020, would be to create a robotic copy of a human body, an android "avatar", controlled entirely by a brain-computer interface. The system would at first be of interest to physically handicapped people, but might also enable people to work in hazardous environments or perform dangerous rescue operations.

DARPA, the American Defense Department Advanced Research Projects Agency, has allotted US$7 million of next year's budget to the development of interfaces enabling a soldier to guide a semi-autonomous machine and allow it to act as the soldier's surrogate.

The second step would be the creation of an autonomous life support Avatar system in which a human brain is transplanted at the end of one's life by 2025. Immobile patients with an intact brain would be able to regain the ability to move via their new synthetic bodies. A varied range of bio-electronic devices might become available, creating superimpositions of electronic and biological systems.

Not a great deal of research is going into this at the moment. The closest match is the research of Dr. Robert J. White who, back in the 1970s, performed several head transplants in monkey (Borghino). They lasted only just a few days because the surgery included severing the spine at the neck, so that the subjects were all paralyzed from the neck down. The animals were euthanized after being studied.

The third step is to occur in the periods from 2030 to 2035. Itskov aims to reverse-engineer the human brain and find a means of "downloading" human personality and consciousness into a synthetic version. This would allow the creation of a human-like artificial intelligence and the achievement of cybernetic immortality for humans.

Although there is much interest among neuroscientists in better understanding the inner workings of the brain, no current research project is yet considering transferring human consciousness into a silicon chip. A robotic arm that can execute the electrical signals of single neurons is certainly a step in that direction.

For the fourth and final step, to occur by the year 2045, Itskov expects to see "substance-independent minds" uploaded not only onto a computer chip, but also into bodies of different compositions. A holographic body could walk through walls or move at the speed of light, while a body made of nanorobots would be able to take on a number of different forms at will. By that time humanity will have made a fully managed evolutionary transition and become a new species.

Itskov is absolutely serious about his project and has invested plenty of his own money, hiring 30 scientists to achieve his goal. The initiative has also received the support and blessing of the Dalai Lama.

2.4 Obstacles to Reaching the Singularity

A number of factors, that may impede the advent of the Singularity, has been proposed. First, as Benjamin Jones (2005) has argued, there is a "Knowledge Burden", or information overload, even when irrelevant information is filtered away. The burden acts as a brake to accelerating technological and economic progress. The knowledge burden is increasing, and has negative consequences for economic growth.

The reason is that with an accumulating stock of knowledge due to technological progress, the expanding time costs of education is delaying the onset of active careers in innovation. By standing on the shoulders of giants, one can see farther, but first one has to climb up their backs. The greater the existing stock of knowledge, the harder this climb becomes. Innovators can compensate by seeking narrower expertise (this is the so-called "the death of the Renaissance Man" effect, i.e. the decline of the multi-talented person), but this may reduce their individual capacity to innovate and force innovators to work in teams.

Empirical evidence that Jones presents, shows that over the course of the 20th century, the mean age at which great inventors and Nobel Prize winners produced their great innovations increased by 6 years. The age at first innovation is trending upwards by 0.6 years per decade. There is a 6 % increase in specialization every ten years and research team size is increasing at the steep rate of 17 % per decade. The decrease observed in patents per American R&D worker of about 50 % since 1975 is accompanied by a rise in team size over that period.

Second, knowledge and skills are *unevenly distributed* and their exponential growth also leads to exponential growth of differences. Although there is diffusion of information between those who have lots of knowledge and those who do not, this transfer becomes less and less effective as the differences widen on the approach to Singularity.

This may already be happening in the scientific community. An article in the August 1995 issue of Scientific American ("Lost Science in the Third World") discusses how third world scientific journals have become essentially invisible to the mainstream, first-world scientific community due citation services and reviewer prejudices. Because of economic constraints, the third world cannot afford many important scientific journals, and the Internet is slow to spread and expensive. This gap is self-reinforcing, and there is a risk that accelerating progress would make it impossible to close.

The possibility that the Singularity occurs for a very limited subset of humanity (a "spike" as opposed to a "swell") cannot be ruled out. This would create a tremendous knowledge and ability gap with unpredictable social, political and economic effects. In the past we have often seen that the have-nots rebel against the elite due to real or imagined grievances, but this time the elite has a real chance of being so advanced that revolt is impossible. Moreover, the more quickly a small group advances, the more likely it is that their attitudes and vision of the world will be strengthened, filtering away information that does not fit their attitudes, leading to groupthink. It may also trigger political tension between the technological haves and have-nots, which could lead to costly conflicts.

Third, there is the matter of *human resistance to change*. Even if a new technology is very useful, there is often a long delay before it becomes widely used, often simply because it is not perceived as necessary or as valuable as it actually is. It took over 140 years (!) for the fax machine to become common and several decades for computers and television to develop to the point where they became extensively usable. Sometimes, more inefficient systems remain "locked in" even when better alternatives are present (for example, practically all English speakers use QWERTY-keyboards instead of the faster and less tiring DVORAK-keyboards) as technologies become more entrenched and where shifting to new systems appears more difficult than continuing with the old. Furthermore, to move to a wholly new technology, an entirely new infrastructure has to be built. This can be slow and expensive. Complicating the matter, as Acemoglu and Robinson (2012) argue, elites often have an interest in limiting the spread of new technology that limits their power. This has served to keep much of the world poor historically.

Fourth, the motivation to innovate may be deceasing since, as technological progress increasingly satisfies current human needs, individuals become less concerned with technological development. They may turn more toward personal growth, unique experiences, and other activities. While such activities may be creative, they are less obviously innovations in a technological sense.

Fifth, there are challenges of coordination. Singularitarians often claim that a few key technologies need to be developed, and then everything will start snowballing. Overlooked is the huge interdependence of technological systems. It is not enough to have the technological ability in one area. Other areas have to be sufficiently developed to lead to major breakthroughs.

Sixth, physical limitations to the Singularity exist. The speed of light prevents the exchange of information quickly over long distances. To communicate faster we have to move closer. There are also limits on information density. The *Bekenstein Bound* states that in computer science there is a maximum information-processing rate for a physical system that has finite size or energy. The speed of molecular or sub-atomic switches also places limitations on possible processing units and memories. Even very advanced civilizations will be subject to the laws of physics.

Seventh, technology forecasters assume that past trends will simply continue indefinitely. However, technology is not (yet) a self-generating force progressing by its own internal dynamics. All known natural growth paths follow a logistic function, which can be approximated by an exponential only in its early stages. Even Kurzweil admits that his exponential growth curves will eventually turn into S-curves, though this would happen a very long time in the future.

Eighth, there are economic incentives to slow down innovation. The first mass produced nanobots are unlikely to be self-produced, if only because the original designer and manufacturer of self-reproducing machines would be destroying its own future market. This self-reproducibility will be a major obstacle to investment. Furthermore, the risk associated with investment on a large scale will not be undertaken until the products and processes are thoroughly tested and the applications are well-established. Extrapolating technology forecasts depend on questionable sustained trends in enabling technologies and continued declining costs. Moreover, old technologies may resist displacement by new technologies because of the large prior investment in the infrastructure supporting them.

Nineth, it is unclear that there will always be demand for new technology: Kurzweil has based his entire structure of expectations on *Say's Law* which states that the supply of a new product creates its own demand. Say's law has been discredited within the economics profession by periods of low demand, such as the Great Depression of the 1930s and the troughs of later business cycles.

Tenth, not all aspects of intelligence are subject to potential increases in productivity. Kurzweil considers what the brain does as a computational exercise. In his opinion, since machines do computations very well, it will become possible to imitate what the brain does with machines. Kurzweil predicts that the computational capacity needed to emulate human intelligence will be available in less than two decades. However, the problem is that productivity increases are less obviously applicable to the other functions of the brain: the emotional, the memorial, the problem solving, the creative and so on. Indeed, most of the energy a human neuron consumes is devoted to maintaining its life support functions rather than its informational processing capabilities.

3 Artificial Intelligence

Artificial Intelligence represents the most plausible path to reaching the Singularity. Charles Darwin (1859) has shown how a complex and adaptive system can arise from an evolutionary process of natural selection acting on random variation without the assistance of an intelligent designer. However, since ancient times humanity has been intrigued by the ability to design intelligent machines. Today, with the advent of the computer and 50 years of research into Artificial Intelligence programming techniques, the dream of creating smart machines is becoming a reality. At this moment in history human biological evolution is on the verge of being superseded by technological progress. Researchers are creating systems which can mimic human thought, understand speech, beat the best human chess player, and countless other feats never before thought possible. Militaries are applying AI logic to their hi-tech systems, and in the near future Artificial Intelligence will noticeably impact our lives.

One of the goals of Artificial Intelligence is to replicate human intelligence in machines or computers. Although until now intelligence has been considered irrelevant to cosmological events and processes, proponents of AI argue that it is more powerful than all other forces in the universe. It may be only a matter of a few centuries before intelligence can manipulate matter and energy and create the universe it wants.

Human intelligence, according to mainstream thinking in psychology, is not a single ability or cognitive process, but rather an array of separate components: learning, reasoning, problem-solving, perception, and language comprehension. Intelligence is the ability to adapt one's behavior to fit new circumstances. Some researchers in AI take a narrower view, and consider human intelligence as only the computational part of the ability to achieve goals in the world. This consists of the ability to solve problems, think quickly, act with purpose, think rationally and associate effectively with the environment.

Intelligence demands a number of irreducible features and capabilities. It requires senses to obtain features from the world and a coherent means for storing the knowledge thereby obtained. Systems of artificial intelligence must be able to process temporal data as patterns in time and store them in a way that facilitates concept formation and generalization. Such knowledge also needs to be automatically adjusted and updated on an ongoing basis, and new knowledge must be appropriately related to existing data. AI systems must be capable of acquiring knowledge on their own. They need to control what input data is processed—where to obtain data, in how much detail, and in what format. Since reality presents more data than is relevant, general intelligence must cope with an overabundance of data, and select the input data used for analysis and learning. It is also important to obtain multiple views of reality. Much of its learning must be autonomous, without teachers, through self-directed learning and adaptation. A general AI system must be able to dynamically and adaptively interact with the environment.

Many researchers do not believe that general artificial intelligence is possible and they concentrate their efforts on domain-specific AI projects for commercial or academic purposes with more immediate results. Nevertheless, General AI promises to make an important contribution toward developing software and robotic systems that are more usable, intelligent, and human-friendly. Probably the closest work that aims to achieve general rather than niche intelligence is the *Novamente project* under the direction of Ben Goertzel (see Goertzel and Pennachin 2007).

3.1 Definition of Artificial Intelligence

Definitions of artificial intelligence fall into two main categories. On the one hand there are systems that *think and act like humans*. These are machines with minds performing activities such as decision-making, problem solving and learning, which require intelligence. These kinds of definitions measure success in terms of fidelity to human performance. On the other hand there are systems that measure success against an *ideal concept of intelligence*, in which a system is intelligent if it takes the best possible action given what it knows. These systems use computational models that make it possible to perceive, to reason and to act.

Although there is no consensus definition of intelligence, there *is* wide agreement among AI researchers that intelligence is required to do the following things: reason, use strategy, solve puzzles, make judgments under uncertainty; represent knowledge, including commonsense knowledge; plan; learn; communicate in natural language; and integrate the use of all of these skills towards common goals. Other important capabilities to be included in the concept of AI are the ability to sense and the ability to act (for example to move and manipulate objects) in the outside world. This includes an ability to detect and respond to hazards. Some sources consider "salience", the capacity for recognizing importance and to evaluate novelty, as an important feature. Some interdisciplinary approaches to intelligence also emphasize the need to consider imagination (taken as the ability to form mental images and concepts that were not programmed in) and autonomy. Computer based systems that exhibit some of these capabilities (e.g., computational creativity, decision support systems, robots, evolutionary computational ability, intelligent agents) do exist, but not yet at a human level. Other aspects of the human mind that are relevant to the concept of AI are the following. *Consciousness* is to ability to have subjective experience and thought. Self-awareness is the capacity to be aware of oneself as a separate individual, especially to be aware of one's own thoughts. Sentience is the ability to "feel" perceptions or emotions subjectively). Sapience is the capacity for wisdom. When a machine can persuasively argue on its own that it has feelings that need to be respected it can be postulated that a machine has consciousness. Although an AI system might be able to bootstrap itself to higher and higher levels of intelligence by thinking about AI, the level of AI at which this process can begin exceeds the current level.

The term Artificial Intelligence was coined in 1956 by John McCarthy, an American computer and cognitive scientist, who organized the first international conference on AI at Dartmouth, New Hampshire. He defined AI as the science and engineering of making intelligent machines, which exhibit reasoning, knowledge, planning, learning, communication, perception and the ability to move and manipulate objects.

Wikipedia defines Artificial Intelligence as the intelligence of machines and the branch of computer science that aims to create it. A modern, widely-used definition describes the field as the study and design of *intelligent agents* where an intelligent agent is a system that perceives its environment and takes actions that maximize his chances of success.

Artificial Intelligence can also be defined as the science of making computers do things that require intelligence when done by humans. Computers are considered to be the right kind of machine to be made intelligent. Computers may be programmed to simulate intelligence. Computer programs have plenty of speed and memory. However, their abilities are limited to those intellectual mechanisms that program designers understand well enough to code into programs.

In this manuscript, the term Artificial Intelligence is used in a very broad sense. It includes, but is not limited to, machine learning, pattern recognition, cognitive architectures, logical models, robot brain architectures, vision, sensor informatics and knowledge engineering.

3.1.1 Turing Test

Alan Turing, in a seminal paper entitled *Computing Machinery and Intelligence* (1950), reduced the problem of defining intelligence to a simple question about *conversation*. In order to verify a machine's capability to demonstrate intelligence, Turing developed a test. Turing asked the question "Can a Machine Think?" Turing's suggestion was that, if the responses from a computer were indistinguishable from those of a human, the computer could be said to be thinking and should be classified as intelligent. Turing concluded: *If a machine* **acts as** *intelligently as a human being, then* **it is** *as intelligent as a human being.*

The Turing Test involves a machine in one room and a person in another, each responding by teletype to remarks made by a human judge in a third room for some fixed period of time. The judge engages in a natural language conversation with the human and the machine and each of them try to appear human; if the judge cannot reliably tell which is which, then the machine is said to pass the test. Hence, being intelligent is defined as passing the Turing Test.

The Turing test has been criticized because it is anthropomorphic in the sense that it attributes human characteristics to non-human animals or non-living things. But there is no reason why intelligent machines should closely resemble humans. Another disadvantage of the Turing test is that it does not test for particular human features such as the ability to be insulted or the temptation to lie. Moreover, a computer might score high when the questioner poses questions which require answers in terms of "Yes" or "No". But a computer may not be expected to perform like a human being to questions of a broad-based, conversational nature, especially in the case of emotionally charged or socially sensitive issues. In some cases, like a search engine, a computer may perform much better and faster than a human so that the questioner can easily tell which is which.

Turing's Test has been confronted with nine common objections (Stanford Encyclopedia of Philosophy 2003). These encompass all of the major criticism against AI. Turing countered that none of these negate the validity of his test.

1. *Theological Objection*: Thinking is a function of man's immortal soul and therefore a machine cannot think. Turing's answer was that God could have granted a computer a soul if He so wished.
2. *Heads in the Sand Objection*: The consequences of machine thinking are too terrible. Hopefully they cannot do so. Turing's answer was that this confuses what *should not* be with what *can or cannot* be.
3. *Mathematical Objection*: There are limits to what questions a computer system can answer. Turing suggested that humans are too often wrong themselves and are pleased at the fallibility of a machine.
4. *Argument from Consciousness*: Not until a machine can write a sonnet or compose a concerto could a machine equal a brain. *Turing answered* by saying that we have no way of knowing whether any being other than ourselves experiences consciousness or emotions.
5. *Arguments from various disabilities*. These arguments all have the form "a computer will never do X".
   (a) *A machine cannot make mistakes*. Turing noted it is easy to program a machine to appear to make a mistake.
   (b) *A machine cannot be self-aware*. Turing asserted that a program which can report on its internal states and processes can certainly be written.
   (c) *A machine cannot have much diversity of behavior*. Turing answered that with enough storage capacity, a computer can behave in an astronomical number of different ways.

6. *Lady Ada Lovelace's Objection*[1]: Computers are incapable of originality because they are incapable of independent learning. Turing's response was that computers can still surprise humans, especially in cases where the consequences of different facts are not immediately recognizable.
7. *Argument from continuity in the nervous system*: According to modern neurological research the brain is not digital. The exact timing and probability of pulses have analog components. Turing's *answe*r was that given enough computing power any analog system can be simulated to a reasonable degree of accuracy.
8. *Argument from the informality of behavior*: Any system governed by laws (such as machines) will be predictable and hence is not truly intelligent. Turing's answer was that this confuses laws of behavior with general rules of conduct. On a broad enough scale, machine behavior can become very difficult to predict.
9. *Extra-Sensory Perception* such as telepathy, clairvoyance, precognition and psychokinesis might not hold for machines. Turing's answer was that conditions can be created in which this would not affect the test and so this argument may be disregarded.

Turing was optimistic that computers would soon be able to exhibit apparently intelligent behavior, answering questions posed in English and carrying on conversations. However, as of 2008, no computer has passed the Turing Test. Trying to pass the Turing Test is not an active focus of much mainstream academic or commercial activity. AI researchers have devoted little attention to passing the Turing test, since there are easier ways to test their programs, such as by giving them a task directly, rather than through the roundabout method of first posing a question in a chat room populated with machines and people. Indeed, Turing never intended his test to be used as a real, day-to-day measure of the intelligence of AI programs. He wanted to provide a clear and understandable example to help discussion of the philosophy of AI.

The Turing test is commonly cited in discussions of artificial intelligence as a proposed criterion for machine consciousness; it has provoked a great deal of philosophical debate. For example, Dennett and Hofstadter (1981) argue that anything capable of passing the Turing test is necessarily conscious, while Chalmers (1995) argues that a philosophical zombie could pass the test, yet fail to be conscious.

Even if the Turing Test is a good operational definition of intelligence, it may not indicate that a machine has consciousness, or that it has intentionality. Perhaps intelligence and consciousness are such that neither one necessarily implies the other. This issue is taken up in Sect. 5.8.

An obvious difficulty with the test is its reliance on the decision by a human judge. The human judge may be unfairly chauvinist in rejecting genuinely intelligent machines or he may be overly liberal in accepting cleverly-engineered mindless machines.

---

[1] Augusta Ada King, Countess of Lovelace (1815–1852) is sometimes considered the World's First Computer Programmer. She was the only legitimate child of the poet Lord Byron. She foresaw the capability of computers to go beyond mere calculating or number-crunching.

There is an ongoing $10,000 *bet* between Mitch Kapor, the founder of Lotus Development Corporation and the designer of Lotus 1-2-3, and Ray Kurzweil about whether a computer will pass a Turing test by 2029. Kurzweil has predicted that Turing-test-capable computers would be manufactured around 2029. The *Loebner Prize* is the first formal Turing test. Hugh Loebner has pledged a Grand Prize of $100,000 and a Gold Medal for the first computer whose responses were indistinguishable from a human's, as evaluated in a competition in which a judge asks questions to humans and computer competitors. In 1991, when the first Loebner prize competition was run, *The Economist* reported that the winning entry incorporated deliberate errors to fool the judges into believing that it was human. This technique has remained a part of the subsequent Loebner prize competitions, and has come to be known as Artificial Stupidity.

Since 2001, another annual competition, started by Chatter Box Challenge (CBC), awards prizes annually to the most humanlike chatterbox, a computer program whose aim is to fool the user into thinking that the program's output has been produced by a human.

3.1.2 Chinese Room Argument

The Chinese Room argument, devised by John Searle, an American philosopher, (1980), is an argument against the notion that a computer capable of passing the Turing test would necessarily be able to think. His argument proceeds as follows. Suppose the Turing test is conducted in Chinese rather than English, and suppose a computer program successfully passes it. Does the system that is executing the program understand Chinese? Searle's argument centers on a thought experiment, in which someone who knows only English sits alone in a room full of boxes of Chinese symbols (a data base), together with a book of instructions for manipulating the symbols (the program). People outside the room send in other Chinese symbols which, unknown to the person in the room, are questions in Chinese. By following the instructions of the program the man in the room is able to pass out Chinese symbols which are correct answers to the questions (the output). From the outside, it will appear that the Chinese room contains a fully intelligent person who speaks Chinese. But there is no one (or anything) in the room that understands Chinese. The instruction book is certainly not aware. Hence, Searle concludes that the Chinese room, or any other physical symbol system, cannot have a mind and that no understanding is created by running a program. The program enables the person in the room to pass the Turing Test for understanding Chinese, but actually he does not understand a word of Chinese.

3.1.3 Ned Block's Blockhead Argument

A second argument against the Turing Test as a standard for intelligence is Ned Block's (an American Philosopher) Blockhead argument. Block (1981) argues that a non-intelligent system can actually be made to pass the Turing Test. Like Searle, Block argues that there is only a finite set of grammatically and syntactically correct responses to any input from a human judge. Although the number of such responses is huge, it is still theoretically possible to program a computer with each of these potential responses. Such a machine can converse with a human on any topic, if it already has all the possible replies pre-programmed in. Hence, the machine would be able to pass the Turing test despite the fact that it fails to possess any actual intelligence.

Behaviorists argue that if something acts conscious in every way, it necessarily is conscious, because they define consciousness in terms of behavioral capacity. Block argues that two systems may be alike in many behavioral properties, yet there could be a difference in the internal information processing that mediates their stimuli and responses. One system could not be intelligent at all, while the other is fully intelligent.

3.2 Scope and Approaches of Artificial Intelligence

AI research is highly technical and specialized, and sharply divided into branches that often fail to communicate with each other. Subfields have grown up around particular academic institutions, the work of individual researchers, the solution of specific problems, longstanding opinions about how AI should be done, and the application of specific tools. General Artificial Intelligence (AGI), or "strong AI", combining all these skills and exceeding human abilities, is still among the field's long term goals. However, at the present time, there is no established unifying theory that guides AI research. Researchers disagree about many issues.

A basic question is whether *a machine can display general intelligence*. How does one know whether a machine *is really* thinking as a person thinks or is just *acting like* it is thinking? Many AI researchers take the position that is summarized in the statement of the Dartmouth Conferences of 1956, which is widely considered as the birth of AI:

> Every aspect of learning or any other feature of intelligence can be so precisely described that a machine can be made to simulate it.

This issue can ultimately be resolved in one of two ways. On the one hand, it may be shown that there is some practical limit to the abilities of computers or that there is some special quality of the biological human mind, which is necessary for thinking, that cannot be duplicated by a machine. On the other hand, it may be shown that such an AI system is possible. If the human nervous system obeys the laws of physics and chemistry, then it should be feasible to reproduce the behavior of the nervous system with some physical device.

In 1963, Alan Newell and Herbert Simon argued that the essence of both human and machine intelligence is *symbol manipulation*. They claimed that a symbol system is necessary and sufficient for intelligence and for machines to be intelligent. They wrote: "A physical symbol system has the necessary and sufficient means of general intelligent action."

This position has been criticized by American philosopher Dreyfus (1992), who argued that human intelligence and expertise depend primarily on unconscious intuitions, rather than conscious symbol manipulation. He claims that these unconscious skills would never be captured in formal rules. Nevertheless, progress has been made towards discovering the rules that govern unconscious reasoning. Neural networks, evolutionary algorithms, and so on are often directed at simulating unconscious reasoning and learning. AI research has generally moved away from symbol manipulation and toward new models that are intended to capture more of human *unconscious* reasoning.

The question of whether a machine can have a mind, consciousness, and mental states, revolves around a requirement proposed by Searle for strong AI: "A physical symbol system, a machine, can have a mind and mental states and is actually thinking." This position may be distinguished from what he called weak AI: "A physical symbol system can act as if it were intelligent."

Strong AI would require a machine to exhibit consciousness and emotions. *Consciousness* is self-awareness, possessed by a machine that is the subject of its own thought. Viewed in this way a program can be written for a machine that can report on its own internal states, such as a debugger. A related issue is whether a machine can process *qualia*, a term used in philosophy to describe *subjective conscious experiences*. Qualia are purely subjective sensory qualities like "the redness of red" that accompany our perception. If two people see the same thing, they may have a different experience. If qualia exist, then a normally sighted person who sees red, would be *unable to describe* the experience of this perception, in such a way that a listener who has never experienced color would be able to know everything there is to know about that experience.

What is mysterious and fascinating about consciousness is not so much *what* it is but *how* it arises: how does a lump of fatty tissue and electricity in a human body give rise to the familiar experience of perceiving, meaning or thinking? This is the *hard problem of consciousness*: explaining the relationship between physical phenomena, such as brain processes, and experience. How can physical processes be accompanied by experience?

Emotions are another highly controversial topic, and are related to consciousness. The question of whether a machine can actually feel emotion, or whether it merely acts as if feeling an emotion, is the philosophical issue of consciousness of machines in another form.

AI is often defined as a field of computer science that explores complex computational models of problem solving by human beings. Computational modeling requires a mathematical and logically formal representation of a problem. Representation is defined as substitution, standing for something else, and it acts as an intermediary between the subject and the objects it observes. Representations serve as a causal connection, as a mediating entity between stimuli and responses. They make thinking possible. Examples of representations are linguistic symbols, mathematical symbols, visual patterns, images, categories, beliefs, propositional attitudes, schemata, and networks.

Certain mental states such as pain, fears or depression may not be representational and may not be suitable for a computational treatment. Many AI researchers are *computationalists*, who believe that the brain is nothing more than a computer, and that consciousness and intelligence are the result of physical processes in the brain. The proponents of this computational theory of mind claim that the relationship between mind and brain is similar, if not identical, to the relationship between a running computer program and the computer it is running on. According to this view human intelligence is nothing more than a form of calculation. This has the implication that artificial intelligence is possible. Continuing progress in the development of faster, more capable computers would cause the computer to equal and then to surpass humans in intelligence. However, this ignores the difficult philosophical question of whether a computer program, running on a digital machine that shuffles the binary digits of zero and one, can duplicate the ability of neurons to create minds, with mental states such as understanding or perceiving, as well as the experience of consciousness.

Moravec's paradox refers to the striking fact that high-level reasoning requires very little computation, while low-level sensorimotor skills require enormous computational resources. Moravec (1988), an Austrian futurist, known for his work on robotics and AI, observed that "it is comparatively easy to make computers exhibit adult level performance on intelligence tests or playing checkers or chess, and it is difficult or impossible to give them the skills of a one-year-old when it comes to perception and mobility." The mental abilities of a four-year-old—recognizing a face, lifting a pencil, walking across a room, answering a question—are some of the hardest engineering problems to be solved.

In this respect, linguist Steven Pinker writes "As the next generations of intelligent devices appear, it will be the stock market analysts and petrochemical engineers who are in danger of being replaced by machines. The gardeners, receptionists, and cooks are secure in their jobs for decades to come." Skills that appear effortless may be difficult to reverse-engineer, but skills that require much effort and study may not necessarily be difficult to engineer at all (Minsky 1988). Indeed, perhaps the most difficult human skills to reverse engineer are those that are unconscious.

From the very beginning, development of automated methods for AI planning has been part and parcel of AI research. Intelligent systems must be able to plan, that is, to determine appropriate actions for their perceived situation. They then must execute them, and monitor the results. Intelligent agents must be able to set goals and achieve them. Algorithmically, a planning problem has, as an input, a set of possible courses of action, a predictive model for the underlying dynamics, and a performance measure for evaluating the courses of action. The output or solution is one or more courses of action that satisfies the specified requirements for performance. A planning problem thus involves deciding "what" actions to do, and "when" to do them.

In classical planning problems, where the environment is static and deterministic, the planner has complete information about the current state of the world. More recently, substantial attention is being paid to planning in environments that are stochastic, dynamic, and only partially observable, which do not satisfy classical planning assumptions. The problem of representing, understanding, and controlling the behavior of agents (or other systems) in the context of incomplete or incorrect information has demonstrated its feasibility in the field of *plausible reasoning*. Multi-agent planning uses the cooperation and competition of many agents to achieve a given goal.

Rapid AI development is occurring in speech recognition. Computerized speech has already arrived and is commercially available. Cell phones enhance the use and appeal of the mobile Internet by allowing users to call up any Web page from a mobile device just by speaking its address. Voice recognition also has security applications. It can properly identify a user, which is a necessity when providing access to corporate or private databases over the Internet. Speech recognition's natural successor, natural language processing, is still poorly developed. However, developments, such as automated language translation, are advancing quickly.

Perhaps the most ambitious examples of AI development that are currently ongoing, relate to *computer learning*. The aim of computer learning is to reason in a variety of ways, learn from experience, and adapt to surprises. Programs exist which can be said to primarily reason. Automated reasoning helps produce software which allows computers to reason completely or nearly completely, automatically. Other reasoning programs are based on heuristic classification. These AIs have found their way into the cockpits of fighter jets, where their main role is to reduce the workload on the pilot by providing advice in certain stressful situations.

Recent AI research defines *intelligent agents*. An "agent" is something which perceives and acts in an environment. A "performance measure" defines what counts as success for the agent. If an agent acts to maximize the expected value of a performance measure based on past experience and knowledge then it is intelligent. The disadvantage of this standard is that it fails to differentiate between "things that think" and "things that do not". By this definition, even a thermostat has intelligence. A few families of intelligent systems already have broad applicability across a wide range of sectors (Arnall 2003).These are intelligent simulation systems, intelligent information resources, intelligent project coaches, and robots.

1. *Intelligent Simulation Systems*

An Intelligent Simulation System (ISS) may be generated to learn more about the behavior of an original system, when the original system is not available for manipulation. The modeling of climate systems is a good example. An ISS may also be employed for training purposes in anticipation of dangerous situations, when the cost of real-world training is prohibitive. Such technologies are particularly well advanced in military applications through the simulation of war 'games'. Another very big business in the realm of ISSs is the videogame market, in which a ISS creates a sense of reality for the game-player.

2. *Intelligent Information Resources*

Intelligent systems may provide access to a wide variety of information, including visual and audio data, with 'data mining' receiving much attention. Data mining is used to extract general regularities from online data. Commercial and government institutions are now logging huge volumes of data and require the means to optimize the use of these vast resources. AI can look for patterns in the data that human users might not look for.

3. *Intelligent Project Coaches*

Intelligent project coaches can function as co-workers, assisting and collaborating in a wide range of teams. 'Interface agents' are computer programs that employ AI techniques to provide active assistance to a user for computer-based tasks. These agents acquire their competence by learning from the user as well as from agents assisting other users. For example, in the US, start-ups are marketing software tools that learn individual users' buying patterns and make personalized recommendations accordingly.

3.2.1 Embodied Artificial Intelligence

Embodiment, the hosting of an AI agent in a physical body, which the AI agent can manipulate, is nowadays considered by many researchers a *condition sine qua non* for any form of intelligence. Pfeifer and Scheier (1999), for example, argue that "intelligence cannot merely exist in the form of an abstract algorithm but requires a physical instantiation, a body". This contrasts with the traditional view that Artificial Intelligence is a computational process, encompassing only disembodied tasks, such as abstract problem solving and reasoning, knowledge representation, theorem proving, formal games like chess, search techniques, and natural language.

By the mid 1980s, the classical computational approach had brought forward many successes in terms of computer and engineering applications: clever machine learning algorithms, text processing systems which utilize matching algorithms, controls for appliances using fuzzy logic, embedded systems (as they are employed in fuel injection systems, breaking systems, air conditioners, etc.), control systems for elevators and trains, natural language interfaces to directory information systems, translation support software, etc.

Until the late 1980s, in cognitive science generally, but particularly in artificial intelligence, the *logic paradigm* prevailed. The assumption was that reasoning amounted to the mechanical manipulation of abstract symbols. The mind was an abstract machine, manipulating symbols by algorithmic computation in the way a computer does. All meaning arose via correspondences between symbols (words, mental representations) and things in the external world. These symbols formed internal representations of external reality, independent of any limitations of the human body, the human perceptual system, and the human nervous system. Human thought was seen as abstract and disembodied. The brain was merely a specific instance of a computing engine which, in principle, could be replaced by a computer, and computers could do anything that brains could do. Machines that mechanically manipulate symbols that correspond to things in the world were believed to be capable of meaningful thought and reason.

Such approaches to knowledge, which models intelligence as disembodied symbol manipulation, could only lead to simulated rather than to real human intelligence. The reason is that intelligent behavior encompasses not just symbolic manipulation and deductive reasoning, but also interaction with others, attunement to one's surroundings, and awareness of the relationship between oneself and one's world. It also includes creativity, physical coordination, emotion, and countless other behavioral manifestations. Real human intelligence includes all of these dimensions. Creatures (humans and animals) have in common strategies to live and survive in their environment by using their cognitive abilities of intelligence which are shaped by their interactions with the environment.

In the early 1990s, a major paradigm shift occurred, with developments in cognitive science moving towards the inclusion of such dimensions. In particular, the connections between the structure of mental processes and physical embodiment were recognized. This approach, known as *embodied*, or *situated*, cognition treats mental processes as an activity that is structured by the body and how it is situated in its environment—that is, as embodied action. Cognition depends upon the experience of having a body with sensorimotor capacities which is embedded in a biological, psychological, and cultural context. An example of embodied cognition is seen in the area of robotics, where movements are based on the robot's direct and immediate interaction with its environment.

While many researchers now agree that cognition has to be embodied, it is far from clear what kind of body artificial intelligence would have to be equipped with. The claim that intelligence requires a *physical* body is not generally accepted. For example, software systems with no body in the physical sense have been considered to be intelligent, since they 'structurally couple' to their environment (Maturana and Varela 1987). All that is required for a system to be embodied in an environment is that perturbatory channels exist between the two. That means that the environment has the capacity to perturb the system, and that the system has the capacity to perturb the state of the environment.

The disadvantage of this definition is that it is of limited use, because it is not particularly restrictive, and because every system is in one sense or another structurally coupled with its environment. A granite outcrop on the Antarctic tundra is persistently perturbed by the wind, and in turn perturbs the flow of air. Hence, it is an embodied system according to the above definition, but certainly it is not an example of embodied cognition.

Summarizing, proponents of the embodiment approach of AI argue that all aspects of cognition, such as ideas, thoughts, concepts and categories are shaped by aspects of the body. These aspects include the perceptual system, the intuitions that underlie the ability to move, the activities and interactions with our environment, and the understanding of the world that is built into the body and the brain. The argument is that true artificial intelligence can only be achieved by machines that have sensory and motor skills and are connected to the world through a body. With the advent of embodiment, the nature of AI has changed dramatically. It has partially moved out of computer science laboratories and into robotics, engineering and biology labs. Implicit in an embodied view of cognition is that intelligence lies less in the individual brain, and more in the dynamic interaction of brains with the wider world, including the social and cultural worlds that are so central to human cognition.

3.2.2 Enactive Artificial Intelligence

Enactivism may be considered as the most developed model of embodied situated cognition. Enactivism emphasizes the idea that subject and object co-arise. Knowing is inseparable from doing. All knowledge is situated in specific activity bound to a social, cultural and physical context. Activity and learning are tied to the specific situations in which they occur. Therefore, cognition cannot be separated from its context, the activity, people, culture, and language, in which it occurs.

With the publication of the book *The Embodied Mind* by Varela et al. (1991), the enactive paradigm emerged. It argued that thinking and cognition are *grounded* in bodily *actions*: it is not knowledge-as-object but knowledge-as-action. Actions are not simply a display of understanding, but they are themselves understandings. For the enactivist, the cognitive system is a producer of meaning in actions rather than a processor of information.

The basic idea of Enactivism is that living beings that actively generate and sustain themselves enact or bring forth their own domains of value and sense-making. They do so with their sensorimotor activity, and the world and the organisms mutually co-determine one another. Living systems achieve autonomy by acting in some way to adjust to local conditions. This idea is encapsulated in the phrase "Knowing is being in doing." In being, doing, and coming to know, that is, in learning, a system defines the world in which it lives. There are certain types of knowledge, such as knowing how to ride a bicycle, that obviously seem to be the result of action rather than, say, logical analysis.

This enactive approach to mind may be described in terms of five themes, which, taken together, serve as a characterization of enactivism. The themes are embodiment, experience, autonomy, sense-making and co-emergence. For enactivism, cognition is embodied action with the purpose of learning about the world, and then acting on the knowledge gained. Cognition, conceived fundamentally as meaning-generation and sense-making, arises from the sensorimotor coupling between organism and environment.

Enactivism also incorporates a role for history. Each individual's developmental trajectory shapes his understanding of reality. Enactivism tries to understand the regularity of the world we are experiencing at every moment. The world which we experience in our co-existence with others always has the mixture of regularity and mutability that is typical of human experience. Therefore, according to enactivists, cognition is the enactment of a world and a mind on the basis of a history of a variety of actions that a being in the world performs.

Living organisms are autonomous by virtue of their self-generated identity as distinct entities, and they use their experience to build an identity. The establishment of identity entails a relationship between the organism and its environment, which is not predetermined, but rather co-determined by that organism and its environment. The notion of autonomy captures how living beings are internally self-constructive in establishing a boundary between themselves and the world with which they are tightly coupled.

The notion of *agent* is crucially important in Enactivist theory and a change in the structure of the agent occurs through learning, not through an environmental stimulus, but through one's internal structure. For enactivists the same stimulus will not cause the same response in all individuals, because the organism is continuously changing and the response to a stimulus depends on what it has previously interacted with. It is not the environment that determines learning, but the agent itself. The reason is that experiences are understood and interpreted on the basis of the agent's knowledge and prior experiences. It is the agent's knowledge, its structure, or its internal dynamics, that affects its reaction.

Although these considerations are rather vague, *living biology* gives a more precise definition of the living identity. In order to explain the nature of living systems the notion of *autopoiesis* which originated in the work of the Chilean biologists Maturana and Varela in the 1970s, provides a useful framework. This term combines the Greek *auto-* (meaning self) and *poiesis* (meaning creation/production.) An autopoietic system is to be contrasted with an *allopoietic* system, such as a car factory, which uses raw materials to generate a car which is something other than the factory itself. Most industrial production processes are allopoietic. An autopoietic system creates itself, sustains itself and produces itself, whereas an allopoietic system is externally created and produces something other than itself.

The difference between autonomy and autopoiesis is that autopoietic systems must produce their own components in addition to conserving their organization. Autonomous machines need only exhibit organizational closure (in the sense that there are sufficient processes within it to maintain the whole), and they are not required to produce their own components as part of their operation. Autopoiesis requires that the operationally closed network produces and realizes itself as a spatially bounded system.

Sense-making is encountered only by those systems whose being is their own doing. Mere autopoiesis is not sufficient for sense-making. Adaptivity needs to be added to autopoiesis in order to generate sense-making. Autopoietic systems are called *adaptive* if they actively regulate their environmental coupling and if their inner workings have their own endogenous dynamics. A non-adaptive autopoietic system would passively react to stimuli so as to maintain its self-generated identity.

Under the enactive approach, the concepts of autopoiesis and sense-making invoke some notion of *emergence*. The idea of emergence stems from the phenomenon of self-organization. Emergence describes the formation of a novel property or process, arising from the interaction of different existing processes or events. The new level is not only autonomous, exhibiting its own identity and laws of transformation, it also introduces, through interaction with its co-defined context, modulations to the boundary conditions of the processes that give rise to it.

Knower and known, mind and world, stand in relation to each other through mutual specification or dependence. In traditional biological theories, there is adaptive evolution of historical lineages because, "the organism proposes and the environment disposes" (Varela et al. 1991). A more modern view is that lineages are adapting to a "moving target"—an environment that is itself changing. Lineages and environments are changing because changes in one bring about changes in each other. The evolving world environment is evolving partly because organisms are themselves changing.

3.2.3 Generative Artificial Intelligence

Machines are gaining in intelligence and there is no reason to believe that they cannot become smarter than humans. Even before that happens, machine intelligence can be designed to operate more effectively, that is, with less intervention of humans. Eventually, however, machine intelligence has to be able to create its own internal structures and its own thinking automatically. This automation of mental capabilities of machines is what has been called *Generative Artificial Intelligence* (*GAI*).

In contemporary AI, algorithms are used for *convergence to some optimum*. The theory of GAI claims that this is the wrong approach. GAI systems do not look for an optimum to converge to, but for an optimal *generation of possibilities* which can be used by the next system to improve itself. This leads to *dynamically interacting architectures*, in which the sub-components have many feedback mechanisms and interactions. GAI claims that AI research should be focusing on the dynamic creation of interaction mechanisms and feedback loops, instead of focusing on the creation of a fixed topology that is characteristic of most contemporary AI systems.

Contemporary AI uses *the* "Input → Transform → Output" (*ITO*) framework to create intelligent behavior in machines. However, this simple process leads to local optimization procedures which result in fragile and inflexible systems. Working on the basis of the ITO system implies that there is optimization toward a stable end-state with a predictable outcome. As long as the human is the generator of the "transform" part, machines will not be intelligent, but merely display a fraction of the intelligence of their creators. However, the ITO procedure is not outdated. There are many examples in the world that, on a local scale, use ITO mechanisms. But often it is better to find the "global optimum". With the rise of computational power and smarter algorithms, according to Van de Zant (2010), it is now time to change the ITO system and to instead create Generative Science and Generative AI.

One of the most important outcomes of science will be the formation of useful new structures of existing matter and energy. Philosopher De Landa (1991) calls this the tracking of the 'machinic phylum'. The machinic phylum is a broad group of abstract machines that drives evolution. There is an overall set of self-organizing processes, in which a group of previously disconnected elements suddenly reaches a critical point. At this point, group members begin to "cooperate" to form a higher entity. The machinic phylum, the intrinsic self-organizing property that pervades the universe, is older than life on Earth. *Generative science* not only tracks the machinic phylum, but also automates these tracking procedures to generate models. These automated procedures have to be able to learn, in order to generalize on the basis of observations and theories.

The new Generative Science occupies itself with the tracking of the machinic phylum, to find new ways of working with the physical world. Specializations have to be allowed and are an essential feature of GAI, because every machine and every organism has limited resources and capabilities. At a deep level these self-assembling processes share similar mathematical structures, which blur the distinction between organic and non-organic life. Both human and robot bodies would ultimately belong to the machinic phylum.

GAI differs from Generative Science in that GAI can do more than tracking the phylum. GAI would allow a large number of alternative options to solve a certain task. If the options do not satisfy the criterion set out by the system, then it might not be solvable. In some cases, the limitations on the generators should be loosened. This could be interpreted as 'thinking out of the box'.

In GAI there is no single solution, but there are many possible configurations. The goal of the machine is to generate sensible possibilities and track those that make sense. This means using the feedback from the environment as a *sorting mechanism* to learn which possibilities actually work and form the best configuration in the struggle between interacting structures, which are called *meshworks*.

These generated structures posses the same kind of function, which is that they form similar parts of an *abstract search engine*. This search engine consists of many different configurations of the same class or type of instances.

The configurations best adapted to their fluctuating environment become the most powerful. There is not a single 'best' configuration, but there are different possibilities. Their interactions are dynamic, and adapt themselves continuously to changing circumstances. Hence there is a *cyclic flux of many of the generators*, such as daily, seasonal and generational patterns. Although the structure of a settlement changes slowly, when the cyclic flux of the generative processes comes to a halt, any structure depending on the cyclic flux usually deteriorates quickly.

The seeming stability of a structure does not imply that there is little internal activity. The feedback loops created by some of the generators can have (adjustable) control parameters that can steer the generated structures into desired directions. Sorting machines can be interpreted as selection mechanisms searching for preferable values of the control parameters of generators in flux.

The rise of cities, as well as evolution and natural selection are examples of such abstract searching machinery. In these cases the pattern is the same. There are generators, a sorting machine and an abstract searching mechanism.

The focus in this new analysis is on mechanisms which create learning. They do so with a *loopy kind of structure*, which can fold back upon itself in order to create a better one. It is very difficult to create these kinds of learning mechanisms. Environments might be created where these mechanisms can evolve in an open ended manner, e.g., using *evolutionary computation or genetic programming*, which explores the possibilities of creating new patterns with new properties.

This involves a search from a population of solutions, in which a competitive selection weeds out poor solutions. The solutions with high fitness are recombined with other solutions by swapping parts of a solution with another one. This process continues until some convergence criteria are satisfied.

Focusing on the automated creation of networks/meshworks using AI probably means that it will be hard, if not impossible, for humans to understand exactly what goes on in the AI. But using the correct tools it should be possible to steer the development of AI systems.

An example could be a robot which is shown some locations in a building and then starts to wander around. It may only be necessary to store a few points on his pathway to start and then a nearest neighbor algorithm can be used to check where it should go from any position to get to any other one. In such a manner the robot does not create a map, but rather it creates the required network of pathway points on the fly. Using *clustering algorithms* on the pathway points ensures generalization and allows for open ended continuous learning.

Machine intelligence should possess general methods or strategies to find solutions for many types of problems. The reason for this is simple: complex real world problems often require complex solutions. The linear increments of the complexity of the methods used in classical AI do not show general applicability, general intelligence, or intelligent behavior. The intelligent systems of classical AI created by humans are not intelligent, but perform a smart trick. The methods of AI are good at optimization of a solution to a specific problem, but there is no bifurcation principle that allows the AI to grow.

Bifurcation theory studies phenomena characterized by sudden shifts in behavior arising from small changes in circumstances, such as e.g., the unpredictable timing and magnitude of a landslide, the stability of ships at sea and their capsizing, bridge collapse, the flight-or-fight behavior of animals.

Predicting critical transitions is difficult because the state of the system may show little change before the tipping point is reached. Also, models of complex systems are usually not accurate enough to predict reliably where critical thresholds may occur. However, it now appears that certain generic characteristics are present in a wide class of systems as they approach a critical point and this is regardless of differences in the details of each system (Scheffer 2009). Therefore, sharp transitions in a range of complex systems demonstrate common characteristics. Although radical changes may be rare, they are of crucial importance to society and there is a need to identify the mechanisms behind these critical transitions. The question is whether there are generic early-warning signals that may indicate if a critical threshold is approaching. Critical thresholds for transitions have been called *bifurcations* (division into branches), where a system becomes unstable and shifts to the alternative state. As systems approach bifurcation points they tend to show a phenomenon known as "critical slowing down" where a tiny change in conditions can lead to a marked qualitative change in the behavior of a system. Near bifurcation points *the return time to equilibrium* upon a small disturbance increases strongly and this makes it difficult and increasingly slow for the system to restore its previous equilibrium. This phenomenon is known as *critical slowing down.*

As a bifurcation is approached certain changes in the characteristics of fluctuations may take place. One important feature is that the slowing down may lead to *an increase in autocorrelation* in the resulting pattern of fluctuations. This is intuitively simple to understand. Because *slowing down* causes the intrinsic *rates of change* in the system to *decrease*, the state of the system at any given moment becomes *more and more like its past state*. The resulting increase in 'memory' of the system can be measured by looking at *lag*-1 *autocorrelation*, which can be interpreted as slowness of recovery. If the system is driven gradually closer to a *catastrophic bifurcation*, there is a marked *increase in autocorrelation* that builds up long before the critical transition occurs.

Increased variance in the pattern of fluctuations is another possible consequence of critical slowing down as a critical transition is approached. In principle, critical slowing down *could* reduce the ability of the system to track the fluctuations, and thereby produce an opposite effect on the variance. However, *usually* an increase in the variance arises and may be detected well before a critical transition occurs.

In summary, the phenomenon of critical slowing down leads to three possible early-warning signals in the dynamics of a system approaching a bifurcation: slower recovery from disturbances, increased autocorrelation and increased variance.

Under Generative AI, the internal dynamics of the system and the interactions with the environment automatically create unpredictable results and the system learns while executing. From the perspective of Generative AI there is no global optimum, but there are processes that generate possibilities, leading to the next bifurcation and new outcomes.

In GAI the data, the internal mechanisms and the environment lead to the construction of informative, though dynamic, states and processes. This combination of steering by data, internal processes and the environment embeds the machine and its intelligence in the environment. *Context* thus becomes an integral part of the development of intelligent machines. A system developed using GAI principles should be able to adapt itself, to grow mentally, and to optimize itself for tasks. The capacities of such an intelligent machine depend on the initial state, and the history of the system. Small fluctuations in the initial conditions can propagate through the system resulting in different perspectives. Different histories can also result in different perspectives.

One of the tasks of GAI is to find the initial conditions of mental processes which have the greatest probability of developing into the mature machine intelligence that designers (or users) of the intelligent machines desire.

3.3 Applications of Artificial Intelligence

AI research has resulted in an extensive body of principles, representations, algorithms, and spin-off technologies. The focus in this subsection is on applications of weak AI, where considerable effort has resulted in some real-world product success.

3.3.1 Expert Systems

A large area of application of artificial intelligence is in *expert systems*. AI programs that achieve expert-level competence in solving problems in specific task areas by bringing to bear a body of knowledge are called knowledge-based or expert systems. They seek to exploit the skills or knowledge that specialists in particular areas have. Expert systems can be thought of as a computerized consulting device. An expert system is software that uses a knowledge base of human expertise for problem solving, or to clarify uncertainties where normally one or more human experts would need to be consulted.

Expert systems were introduced by researchers in the Stanford Heuristic Programming Project, including the "father of expert systems" Edward Feigenbaum, with the Dendral and Mycin systems. Principal contributors to the technology were Bruce Buchanan, Edward Shortliffe, Randall Davis, William van-Melle, Carli Scott, and others at Stanford. Expert systems were among the first truly successful forms of AI software.

Expert systems are most valuable to organizations that have a highlevel of experience and expertise that cannot be easily transferred among members. Expert systems are designed to carry the intelligence and information found in the intellect of experts and provide this knowledge to other members of the organization for problem-solving purposes. Generally, expert systems are used for problems for which there is no single "correct" solution which can be encoded in a conventional algorithm.

Expert systems have been used to facilitate tasks in the fields of accounting, medicine, process control, financial services, production, human resources, among others. They are also used in engineering and manufacture in the control of robots, where they inter-relate with vision systems.

The most important ingredient in any expert system is knowledge. However, knowledge is almost always incomplete and uncertain. Typically, the problem areas are so complex that a simpler traditional algorithm cannot provide a proper solution. As such, expert systems do not typically provide a definitive answer, but make probabilistic recommendations. One method of operation of expert systems is through a quasi-probabilistic approach with confidence factors or weights, which quantify uncertainty in the degree to which the available evidence supports a hypothesis.

The *internal structure* of an expert system can be considered as consisting of three parts: the knowledge base, the database, and the rule interpreter. The knowledge base captures the knowledge from the expert and holds the set of rules of inference that are used in reasoning. Most of these systems use IF–THEN rules to represent knowledge. Typically, such systems have between a few hundred and a few thousand rules. Because each rule is a unit, rules may be deleted or added without affecting other rules, though these changes can affect which conclusions are reached.

The database gives the context of the problem domain and is generally considered to be a set of useful facts. These are the facts that comprise the condition part of the action rules. In order to simulate the human reasoning process, a vast amount of knowledge needs to be stored in the knowledge base. The rule interpreter is known as an inference engine that uses the rules together to draw conclusions. It controls the knowledge base, using the set of facts, to produce even more facts.

Communication with the system is ideally provided by a natural language interface. This enables a user to interact directly with the intelligent system. Once the system is developed, it is placed in the real world to solve the problem, typically as an aid to human workers or as a supplement to some information system. Expert systems may or may not have learning components. When one finds that the expert system does not produce the desired results, work begins to expand the knowledge base, not to re-program the procedures.

In the past most expert systems have been run only on large information handling systems. The increasing storage capacity of personal computers has made it possible to consider running some types of simple expert systems on them. However, this ability depends on the nature of the application, and the amount of stored information required. Early expert systems required the entire rule base to be stored, since all the rules were, in effect, chained or linked together by the structure of the rule base. However, *segmentation* of the rule base, into contextual segments or units, made it possible to eliminate the portions of the rule base containing data or knowledge that are not needed for a particular application. Segmentation also allows much smaller memory capacities than were possible with earlier arrangements. Of course, provisions must be made to manage various intersegment relationships.

The principal difference between expert systems and traditional problem solving programs concerns the way in which the problem related expertise is coded. In traditional applications, problem-related expertise is encoded in both program and data structures. Under the expert system approach, the problem expertise is mostly encoded in data structures. The program (inference engine) of an expert system is relatively independent of the problem domain and it processes the rules without regard to the problem area they describe.

Real time expert systems are designed to reason over time, and to change conclusions as the state of the monitored system changes. Therefore, these systems must respond to constantly changing input data. The inference engine must track the times of each data input and each conclusion, and propagate new information as it arrives. It must ensure that all conclusions are still current. Facilities for periodically scanning data, acquiring data on demand, and filtering noise, become essential parts of the expert system.

Simple expert systems merely use simple true/false logic to evaluate data. More sophisticated systems are capable of performing some evaluation, taking into account real-world uncertainties. Such sophistication is difficult to develop and still highly imperfect.

Nevertheless, compared to traditional programming techniques, expert-system approaches provide added flexibility and easier modifiability. They have the ability to model rules as data rather than as code. In practice, modern expert-system technology is employed as an addition to traditional programming techniques, and this hybrid approach allows the combination of the strengths of both approaches.

However, an expert system provides no guarantee about the quality of the rules on which it operates. All self-designated "experts" are not necessarily actually expert, and a challenge is to recognize the limits to their knowledge. Furthermore, expert systems are notoriously narrow in their domain of knowledge. An amusing example is a case in which a researcher used a "skin disease" expert system to diagnose his rust bucket car. The system concluded that the car was likely to have developed measles. Expert systems are thus prone to making some errors that humans would easily spot, but also some that may go unnoticed for some time.

An expert system is not optimal for all problems, and considerable knowledge is required to use such a system properly. The ease of rule creation and rule modification can be a double-edged sword. A system can be sabotaged by a non-expert user who can easily add worthless rules, or rules that conflict with existing ones. Many systems fail because of the absence of or the neglect of facilities for system auditing, detection of possible conflict, and rule lifecycle management.

In general, such applications are used to increase the productivity of knowledge workers by intelligently automating their tasks, or to make technical products of all kinds easier to use for both workers and consumers through intelligent automation of their complex functions.

3.3.2 Examples of Applications of AI

There are many interesting applications of artificial intelligence at the present time. A few examples are given here.

Autonomous Planning and Scheduling: A hundred million miles from Earth, NASA's Remote Agent program became the first on-board autonomous planning program to control the scheduling of operations for a spacecraft. Remote Agent generates plans from high-level goals specified from the ground. It monitors the operation of the spacecraft as the plans are executed, detecting, diagnosing, and recovering from problems as they occur.

Game Playing: Deep Blue became the first computer program to defeat the world champion in a chess match when it bested Garry Kasparov by a score of 3.5 to 2.5 in an exhibition match. Kasparov said that he felt a "new kind of intelligence" across the board from him. Newsweek magazine described the match as "The brain's last stand."

Autonomous Control: The computer vision system ALVINN steered a car to keep it following a lane. NAVLAB video cameras transmitted road images to ALVINN, which then computed the best direction to steer, based on experience from previous training runs.

Diagnosis: Medical diagnosis programs have been able to perform at the level of an expert physician in several areas of medicine. For example, in one case, a leading expert on lymph-node pathology scoffed at a program's diagnosis of an especially difficult case, but eventually, the expert agreed with the decision and explanation of machine's program.

Logistics Planning: During the Persian Gulf crisis of 1991, U.S. forces deployed a Dynamic Analysis and Replanning Tool, DART, to do automated logistics planning and scheduling for transportation. This involved up to 50,000 vehicles, cargo, and people at a time, and had to account for starting points, destinations, routes. The AI planning techniques allowed a plan to be generated in hours that would have taken weeks with older methods. The Defense Advanced Research Project Agency (DARPA) stated that this single application more than paid back its 30 year investment in AI.

Robotics: Many surgeons now use robot assistants in microsurgery. Computer vision techniques are used to create a three-dimensional model of a patient's internal anatomy. Robotic control is then applied to guide the insertion of a hip replacement prosthesis.

Language Understanding and Problem Solving: There are computer programs that solve crossword puzzles better than most humans, using constraints on possible word fillers, a large database of past puzzles, and a variety of information sources including dictionaries and online databases.

These are just a few examples of artificial intelligence systems that exist today. It is not magic or science fiction—but rather science, engineering, and mathematics. Ironically, AI is a victim of its own success. Whenever an apparently mundane problem was solved, such as building a system that could land an aircraft unattended, or read handwritten postcodes to speed mail sorting, the problem was deemed by some not to have been AI in the first place. If it works, it can not be AI, was the saying.

The effect of repeatedly moving the goal-posts in this way was that AI came to refer to blue-sky research that was still years away from commercialization. Researchers joked that AI stood for 'Almost Implemented'. Meanwhile, the technologies that worked well enough to make it on to the market, such as speech recognition, language translation and decision-support software, were no longer regarded as AI. Yet all three once fell well within the umbrella of AI research. AI-inspired systems are already integral to many everyday technologies such as internet search engines, bank software for processing transactions and in medical diagnosis.

One measure of the growth of practical applications is the rapid growth in the number of patents mentioning the term *artificial intelligence* and related terms (*knowledge based*, *fuzzy logic*, *expert system*, *genetic algorithm*). Other patents using AI techniques might be classified in an area of application such as medicine. These numbers confirm another important trend: AI technology is more likely to be embedded in some larger system than embodied in a stand-alone system. Successful applications of AI are part of, and buried in, larger systems that probably do not carry the label *AI inside*.

4 Artificial Happiness

Since the dawn of time, humans have sought short-cuts to happiness. The drugs of today promise ecstasy, or the transcending of normal consciousness, in a pill. Neuroscientists are beginning to document the neural correlates of happiness. The future will tell whether artificial intelligence can increase happiness. In principle this could occur in several ways, but two seem most obvious. One way is through a direct channel. Artificially intelligent entities could use their intelligence to develop technologies for producing artificial happiness, much as they could invent methods of achieving Methuselarity. Another channel is indirect. By increasing wealth and living standards, AI could make people happier. We argue in this chapter that, if historical experience is a guide, AI is unlikely to lead to greater happiness through either of these mechanisms.

4.1 What is Happiness?

There is no consensus among experts on the definition of happiness. Some have viewed happiness primarily as a matter of positive emotion. For example, the economist Layard (1980) suggests the following definition: happiness is feeling good, enjoying life, and wanting the feeling to be maintained. This dimension of happiness is sometimes referred to as subjective well being (Diener 1984; Seligman 2002; Kahneman et al. 1999). In recent years, broader definitions have gained acceptance. Haidt (2005) emphasizes the role of relationships: "between yourself and others, between yourself and your work, and between yourself and something larger than yourself". Tal Ben Shahar (2007) defines happiness as "the overall experience of pleasure and meaning." Csikszentmihalyi (1990) includes a notion of flow, or engagement, living and working in fullness, and performing work that enables us to express our uniqueness. He writes, "It is the full involvement of flow, rather than happiness that makes for excellence in life. We can be happy experiencing the passive pleasure of happiness, but this kind of happiness is dependent on favorable external circumstance. The happiness that follows flow is our own making, and it leads to increasing complexity and growth in consciousness." Seligman (2011) proposes the PERMA model, which emphasizes that happiness consists of five components: positive emotion, engagement, relationships, meaning and accomplishment.

4.2 What Makes People Happy?

A large literature has studied the factors that correlate with happiness, and some consistent patterns have emerged (Myers 2007).

Happy people have certain emotional traits: Extraversion, self-esteem, optimism, and a sense of personal control are among the hallmarks of happy individuals. Some of these traits, such as extraversion, are genetically influenced. Like cholesterol level, happiness is affected by genes, yet also somewhat amenable to volitional control.

The type of work and leisure one engages in influences happiness: Mihaly Csikszentmihalyi reports an increased quality of life when work and leisure enlarge one's skills. Between the anxiety of being overwhelmed, and the boredom of being underwhelmed, lies the unself-conscious, absorbed state of *flow*.

Happy people have strong relationships: Humans are social animals, with an obvious need to belong. For most people, solitary confinement results in misery. Having close friends, and being with them, is pleasurable. People who are in good romantic relationships are happier than those who are not. In National Opinion Research Center surveys of more than 42,000 Americans since 1972, 40 % of married adults describe themselves as very happy, in contrast to 23 % of adults who have never been married. The marital happiness gap also occurs in other countries and is similar for men and women.

Those with faith are happier: The same National Opinion Research Center surveys reveal that 23 % of those who never attend religious services report being very happy, in contrast with 47 % of those who attend more than weekly. To explain this pattern, psychologists have pointed out that religious organizations often offer social support, meaning, and assistance in managing the terror of one's inevitable death.

There seems to be a genetic component: Lykken and Tellegen (1996), from the University of Minnesota, studied the role of genes in determining satisfaction in life. From information on 4,000 sets of twins they found that about 50 % of one's satisfaction with life comes from a genetic predisposition. However, neuroscientists have established that the brain is plastic, in that it rewires and changes itself in response to experience. Thus, a genetic predisposition does not mean a particular trait is always expressed or cannot be modified.

Happiness changes over the life cycle: Happiness tends to evolve with age. Self-reported happiness is relatively high in youth and declines until one's reaches his 1940s. It then begins to rise again and continues to rise into old age. Perhaps fittingly, the relationship between happiness and age is smile shaped. Controlling for age, healthy people are happier than sick people.

People are not very good at predicting what will make them happy and how long that happiness (or unhappiness) will last. They expect positive events to make them much happier than those events actually do, and they expect negative events to make them unhappier than they actually do. For example, 73 % of Americans in 2006 answered "yes" when Gallup asked "Would you be happier if you made more money?" However, as we discuss below, the relationship between income and happiness is very weak.

Ed Diener et al. (1985) have shown that the *frequency* of positive experiences is a much better predictor of happiness than is the *intensity* of positive experiences. Diener has shown that how good experiences are does not matter nearly as much as how many good experiences you have. Somebody who has a dozen mildly nice things happen each day is likely to be happier than somebody who has a single truly amazing thing happen. This is consistent with the general findings that specific events create only temporary changes in happiness.

Gilbert (2007) describes a study which measured the happiness of lottery winners and paraplegics. In the short-run, winning the lottery made individuals happier and becoming paraplegic made people less happy. However, surprisingly, they showed no difference in happiness a year after the incident occurred. This means that individuals have a set level of happiness that they tend to revert to regardless of the events they experience.

4.3 The Current State of Artificial Happiness

Currently, unhappiness is mainly fought with pharmacology, which has replaced psychotherapy over the last few decades. More than 15 % of Americans, including 10 % of children, now use anti-depressants, such as Prozac, Zoloft, and Paxil, and the diagnosis of depression is made more and more liberally (Angell 2011). Most antidepressants are *serotonin reuptake inhibitors* (SSRIs), slowing the reabsorption of serotonin by the neurons that release it, so that more remains in the synapses for a longer period of time. The scientific rationale for this type of treatment is *biogenic amine theory*, which claims that happiness is a matter of brain biochemistry and that emotional valence is determined by the chemical imbalance in the brain. If this is the case, then changing the chemical balance in the proper way would increase the happiness of the subject.

However, this claim is in dispute. Ed Diener and others argue that pharmacological routes to happiness merely mask symptoms rather than treat causes. In this regard, antidepressants act like drugs such as alcohol or narcotics, which do not create happiness. They simply alter human consciousness in a way that allows the mind to temporarily change its mood. These drugs work by dampening certain aspects of brain function and creating an altered mental state, so that true reality becomes concealed from a person's consciousness. The dampened brain functions allow a person to imagine an alternate reality that is generally more pleasing. It is by dampening or altering brain functions and by affecting consciousness that alcohol transforms how we feel.

Furthermore, whether antidepressants have anything beyond a placebo effect is in question. Kirsch et al. (2008) reviewed thirty-eight published clinical trials that compared various treatments for depression with placebos, or compared psychotherapy with no treatment. Most these trials lasted for six to eight weeks, and during that time, patients tended to improve somewhat even without any treatment. Kirsch found that placebos were three times as effective as no treatment. Antidepressants were only marginally better than placebos. Placebos were 75 % as effective as antidepressants.

In follow-up research, Kirsch (2010) examined a data set from 42 trials of six antidepressant drugs approved between 1987 and 1999: Prozac, Paxil, Zoloft, Celexa, Serzone, and Effexor. Overall, placebos were 82 % as effective as the drugs, as measured by the Hamilton Depression Scale (HAM-D), a widely used score of symptoms of depression. The results were much the same for all six drugs: they were all equally unimpressive. Yet because the positive studies were extensively publicized, while the negative ones which failed to show effectiveness were hidden, it came to be believed that these drugs were highly effective antidepressants. This practice greatly biased the medical literature, medical education, and treatment decisions.

Moreover, Kirsch observed that even treatments that were not antidepressants, such as synthetic thyroid hormone, opiates, sedatives, stimulants, and some herbal remedies, were as effective as antidepressants in alleviating the symptoms of depression. Kirsch writes "*Antidepressant drugs that increase, decrease, or have no effect on serotonin all relieve depression to about the same degree.*" Kirsch reaches the overall conclusion that antidepressants are probably no more effective than placebos.

Indeed, serotonin reuptake inhibitors may actually be harmful and create a dependency. When an SSRI antidepressant increases serotonin levels in synapses, it stimulates compensatory changes through negative feedback. In response to high levels of serotonin, presynaptic neurons release a smaller quantity, and the postsynaptic neurons become desensitized to it. In effect, the brain is trying to nullify the drug's effects (Whitaker 2010).

Long-term use of psychoactive drugs alters neural function. After several weeks on psychoactive drugs, the brain's compensatory efforts begin to fail, and side effects emerge. These side effects are often treated with other drugs, and many patients end up on a cocktail of psychoactive drugs prescribed for multiple diagnoses. Andreasen et al. (2011) present evidence that the use of antipsychotic drugs is associated with shrinkage of the brain, and that the effect is directly related to the dose and duration of treatment.

Getting off the drugs is exceedingly difficult, according to Whitaker, because when they are withdrawn the compensatory mechanisms are left unopposed. When the drug is withdrawn, serotonin levels fall precipitously because the presynaptic neurons are not releasing normal amounts, and the postsynaptic neurons no longer have enough receptors. The symptoms produced by withdrawing psychoactive drugs are often confused with relapses of the original disorder. This can lead psychiatrists to resume drug treatment, perhaps at higher doses.

4.4 Cosmetic Happiness

There have been several studies in recent years suggesting that people, who undergo cosmetic enhancements, either through surgery or less invasive procedures such as Botox injections, not only experience improved self-esteem but also enhanced mood. Facial expressions have a direct correlation with emotional state. While it is obvious that certain emotions lead to specific facial expressions, causality may also go in the other direction at the same time. In other words, when you look happier, you feel happier. Hence, the question is: should you get Botox injections or undergo cosmetic surgery if you're depressed? Haidt (2006) argues that cosmetic surgery can increase happiness for a long period of time. However, it seems likely that most of the effect is due to the enhancement to ones self-esteem, and the persistent positive feedback from others that is received. Hamermesh and Abreveya (2011) find that the top 15 % of people in terms of attractiveness are 10 % happier than average.

4.5 Synthetic Happiness

Synthetic Happiness is distinct from artificial happiness (Gilbert 2007). Synthetic happiness is the ability (instinctive as well as learned) for a human being to manufacture her own happiness. This is very different from the natural happiness that is based on favorable external events that a human experiences.

One way to understand synthetic happiness is in terms of competing freedoms. Freedom is the friend of natural happiness: *when you get what you want, this is natural happiness*. Freedom to choose, on the other hand, can be considered the enemy of synthetic happiness, because it is *often when you* don't *get what you want* that the potential for manufacturing synthetic happiness comes into play. Dan Gilbert provides the following example of the production of synthetic happiness.

"Imagine a gallery is giving away two free paintings. You are determining which to get and believe you should go with option A, when someone else takes it. So, you take option B instead. You secretly desired A more, but after getting accustomed to B you find that it is a much better choice and are completely happy with the painting your received. This is called synthetic happiness". Although most people tend to think that synthetic happiness will never come close to the feeling of natural happiness, but Gilbert says that this is not the case. Synthetic happiness is perfectly real. Synthetic happiness is what we can produce when we do not get what we want, while natural happiness is what we experience when we do. They have different origins, but they are not necessarily different in terms of how they make us feel.

4.6 Money and Happiness

Research shows that in Western countries, even as per capita GDP has gone up in recent decades, happiness levels have either stayed the same or have decreased. There is some tendency for prosperous nations to have happier and more satisfied people (though these also tend to be countries with high literacy, civil rights, and stable democracies). But the correlation between national wealth and well-being tapers off above a certain level. Countries with high levels of income equality, like Scandinavian countries, have higher levels of happiness than countries with an unequal distribution of wealth, such as the United States, Scandinavian countries have high levels of community integration, which further supports subjective wellbeing.

The happiness of a people does not increase with rising affluence. Citizens of developed nations consume many products that their grandparents of a half century ago seldom knew: air conditioning, the Internet, MP3 players, and bigger houses. Yet they are no happier. Americans' average buying power has almost tripled since the 1950s, while reported happiness has remained almost unchanged. The same is true in other countries, according to economist Easterlin (1974). Economic growth in affluent countries has not demonstrably improved human morale. The same applies to China, where Gallup surveys since 1994 reveal huge increases in the percentage of households with modern items such as color TVs and telephones, but somewhat diminished life satisfaction.

At the individual level, there is no significant relationship between how much money a person makes and how happy they are. Diener and Seligman (2004), interviewed members of the Forbes 400, (the richest Americans), and found that they were only a tiny bit happier than the rest of the population. Indeed, the pursuit of such riches may result in unhappiness. Kasser and Ryan (1993) discovered that people for whom money, success, fame and good looks (extrinsic goals) are especially important are less satisfied than those who strive for good relationships with others, develop their talents and are active in social causes (intrinsic goals).

One explanation of this phenomenon lies in the concept of the *hedonic treadmill*. When we want something and then attain it, we do not seem to be any better off. It is like we are walking on a treadmill but not really getting anywhere because we are adapting to things. Brickman and Campbell (1971) studied lottery winners and found that one year later, life satisfaction was not significantly greater for the winners. This process of adaption explains why we are not significantly happier despite significant increases in the material standard of living over the last 50 years.

Although the correlation between personal income and happiness is surprisingly weak, recent surveys do indicate that across individuals, as across nations, the relationship is curvilinear: the association between income and happiness is positive for poor individuals but tapers off once people have sufficient income to afford life's necessities and a measure of control over their lives.

4.7 Pharmacological Avenues to Intelligence?

The abuse of drugs that are prescribed to treat attention deficits, such as Ritalin and Adderall, is increasing among individuals who want to improve their mental performance. Similar issues arise here as for drugs that treat unhappiness. These drugs do not make you smarter, but temporarily make you perform better on cognitive tasks. They do so by temporarily increasing the level of dopamine in the synapses of dopaminergic neurons, by slowing the reuptake of dopamine after neuronal firing.

The active ingredient in Ritalin is methylphenidate. This compound shares many of the pharmacological effects of amphetamine, methamphetamine, and cocaine. Methylphenidate is now the most commonly prescribed psychotropic medicine for children in the U.S.

Methylphenidate potentially improves the performance of anyone—child or not, ADD-diagnosed or not, on cognitive tasks. On the basis of methylphenidate's recreational appeal, criminal entrepreneurs have responded with interest, resulting in many thefts of methylphenidate at pharmacies and an active secondary market.

4.8 Can Artificial Intelligence Increase Happiness?

Artificial happiness seems difficult to achieve, if the evidence from antidepressant drugs is any guide. The effects on emotion are temporary, treat symptoms rather than causes, and result in dependency. There is no evidence that new technologies can create happiness. Whether artificial intelligence can develop a new technology to increase happiness is an open question. However, such a feat would be a difficult challenge since it would rely on entirely novel technology, rather than improvement upon existing ones.

It also seems unlikely that artificial intelligence could provide a means to increase natural happiness. While robots may provide new and fruitful relationships for many individuals and artificial experiences may provide engagement, it is difficult to see how artificial intelligence might give individuals more meaning in their lives or a sense of accomplishment. In fact, if they replace humans in many of the tasks and types of employment that people find fulfilling, humans might experience less meaning and accomplishment in their lives.

Artificial intelligence promises to raise material living standards. However, the evidence from the past several decades shows that the huge increase in wealth and consumption that has occurred over that period has not increased happiness. There is no reason to suppose that future innovations would be any different. Furthermore, an increase in average wealth may even decrease average happiness if it is accompanied by an increase in income inequality, which would occur if some individuals can profit from it more than others.

5 Issues in Artificial Intelligence

5.1 Competition Between Humans and Computers

In information technology there is a spectrum of processing tasks. At one end are easily automated tasks, requiring straightforward application of existing rules. Such tasks include performing arithmetic to pattern recognition tasks such as in automatic driving in traffic.

At present, embedding human knowledge in software for highly structured situations, such as operating a driverless vehicle, is an enormously difficult task. Popular science has been promising driverless cars since the 1940s. In 2004, economists Frank Levy and Richard Murnane argued that the kind of pattern recognition that driverless cars require was impossible (Ozimek 2012):

> The… truck driver is processing a constant stream of [visual, aural, and tactile] information from his environment…. To program this behavior we could begin with a video camera and other sensors to capture the sensory input. But executing a left turn against oncoming traffic involves so many factors that it is hard to imagine discovering the set of rules that can replicate a driver's behavior…

In that same year, 2004, DARPA held their first Grand Challenge, which asked competing teams to build a driverless car that can make it across 150 miles of dessert. Confirming Levy and Murnane's pessimism, the longest any car made it was 8 miles, and this took several hours.

However, Google has recently made astounding headway in building a functioning driverless car. Its current capabilities are already very impressive, so much so that the state of Nevada recently became the first American state to pass regulations allowing autonomous cars.

A deep aversion to handing over control to a computer may act as an impediment to the driverless car. But it need not be the case that the first time that control is handed over to a robot that it will speed down the interstate at 70 miles-per-hour. Autonomous driving might first be used for slow moving, stop-and-go traffic. A precursor to this can be seen in cars that park themselves. We can ease our way into comfort with it. However, we should have little doubt: driverless cars are in our future.

Complex communication is another example that is hard for machines to emulate especially in emotional or ambiguous situations. In this vein, IBM's Jeopardy! winning supercomputer Watson may be cited as further technological proof that the world is on the cusp of change. The supercomputer Watson, developed at IBM, played the game show Jeopardy. This required the ability to engage in complex communication and pattern matching. It appears that even the best human players could not keep up with the new computer contestant. Watson shows not only more of the impressive pattern recognition seen in driverless cars, but also demonstrates complex language skills that were once thought beyond the province of computers. Supercomputers like Watson will drastically change medicine and other fields of knowledge fields. In fact, IBM and Memorial Sloan-Kettering Cancer Center are already working on teaching Watson to aid in diagnosis and to suggest treatments for cancer.

Therefore, digital pattern recognition abilities have recently advanced rapidly into territory thought to be uniquely human. This remarkable progress can be attributed to Moore's Law, which states that the number of transistors in a minimum-cost integrated circuit doubles every 18 months. It also seems that software can progress at least as rapidly in some domains as hardware does.

As a consequence, according to Basu and Fernald (2008), inexpensive information and communication technology allow departures from business as usual by fostering an ever-expanding sequence of complementary inventions in industries using ICT. Hence, digitization is not a single project providing one-time benefits but it is an ongoing process of creative destruction that will make profound changes at the level of the task, the job, the process and the organization itself.

A popular idea is that the potential for technology makes human labor obsolete. However, this is not at all what happened with technological progress such as during the Industrial Revolution in which more human workers were needed, not fewer. Over time, technological progress creates opportunities in which people compete using machines, and humans and machines collaborate in order to produce more, to capture markets and to compete with other teams of humans and machines. As an example, the best chess players are not computers, nor are they humans; the best chess payers are teams of humans using computers. As Gary Kasparov noted, teams of human plus machines dominate the strongest computers. Weak human + machine + better process is superior to a strong computer alone and superior to a strong human + machine + inferior process.

This pattern applies throughout the economy. The key to winning the competition is not to race against machines, but to win by using machines. Although computers win at routine processing, repetitive arithmetic and error-free consistency, and are becoming better at complex communication and pattern matching, computers have three failings. Computers lack intuition and creativity, they may be fragile in uncertain or unpredictable environments, and they are lost when working outside a predefined domain.

The solution for the implementation of the winning human + machine strategy is organizational innovation that leverages both ever-advancing technology and human skills. Simply substituting machines for human labor rarely adds much value or high returns. It only results in small productivity improvements. In order to create value, what is required is to combine workers with digital technology.

Several especially promising ways of mixing human and machine capabilities are listed by Brynjolfsson and McAfee (2011). They include

1. Combining the speed of technology with human insight;
2. Using technology to test creative human ideas;
3. Leveraging IT to enable new forms of human collaboration and commerce;
4. Using human insight to apply IT and their data to create more effective processes;
5. Using IT to propagate newly developed and improved business processes.

5.2 Threatening Artificial Intelligence

AI is viewed by most people as *scary and threatening* because of the human loss of control over autonomous intelligent machines. One might consider this fear misplaced since AI is still in its infancy and the many currently existing technologies—such as nuclear and biological weapon systems—are far more threatening than anything AI has to offer. However, AI may represent a threat not so much as a technology, but as a social movement in which a rational, scientific world-view prevails over older cultural and religious beliefs. AI machines may destroy us because it is the vehicle through which the world-view of their builders triumphs, changing our notions of who and what we are. In this sense AI is scary to some.

Several critics have argued that AI technology has the potential to disrupt existing society and introduce new dangers and malaise. Nick Bostrom, Teacher and Philosopher at Oxford University, published a paper "Existential Risks" in the Journal of Evolution and Technology (2002). Bostrom states that Artificial Intelligence has the capability to bring about *human extinction*, which is, of course, not what society intends for Artificial Intelligence to do. A well-known movement opposing technological development was the "Luddite" movement which began in 1811 in Nottingham, England, and destroyed many wool and cotton mills until the British government harshly suppressed the movement by making machine breaking a capital crime. The Luddite fallacy has become a precise concept in neoclassical economics, where it refers to the belief that labor-saving technologies, which increase output per worker, would increase unemployment by reducing the demand for labour. The fallacy is that instead of seeking to keep production constant by employing a smaller, more productive workforce, employers increase production while keeping workforce size constant.

The modern incarnations of the Luddites oppose the development of new technologies, and may grow increasingly vocal and radical if the pace of innovations accelerates. Although neo-Luddites might delay the application on some new technologies, the march of technology is irresistible in the long run.

5.3 Friendly Artificial Intelligence

Technology does not always introduce new dangers and risks for human health or the environment. It has always been a mixed blessing, bringing benefits too, such as longer and healthier life spans, freedom from physical and mental drudgery. Artificial intelligence may also be used to benefit humanity. The ethics of artificial intelligence is a part of a broader discussion of the ethics of technology. AI systems with goals that are not perfectly identical to or very closely aligned with human ethics are intrinsically dangerous unless measures are taken to ensure the safety of humanity. A very strong case can be made that, out of all the advanced technologies being debated, Friendly AI is the best technology to develop *first*. A Friendly AI is an AI that takes actions that are beneficial to humans and humanity. Friendliness should be the sole top-level goal ("supergoal") of the AI system. This is consistent with the "precautionary principle" often applied as a criterion in technology policy.

According to the *Precautionary Principle*, if the consequences of a new technology are unknown but, as judged by scientists, have a risk of being negative, it is better to not implement the technology. The burden of the proof that it is not harmful falls on those introducing the new technology. In practice, that principle is strongly biased against technological progress which may be vital to the continued survival and well-being of humanity. An alternative more sophisticated principle that incorporates a more extensive and accurate assessment of options is the *Pro-actionary Principle* which balances all the consequences, good as well as bad, the risks of action and inaction by weighing the opportunity cost of not acting with the new technology and the option value of waiting for further information before acting.

Yudkowsky (2008) of the Singularity Institute for Artificial Intelligence has called for the creation of "Friendly AI", smart enough to improve on its own source code without programmer intervention, to mitigate the existential threat of hostile intelligences. However, the field of AI is not advanced enough to pronounce with certainty that Friendly AI can be created.

Weizenbaum (1976) argued that AI technology should not be used to replace people in positions that require respect and care, such as customer service representatives (AI technology is already used today for telephone-based interactive voice response systems), therapists, nursemaids for the elderly, judges, or police officers. Weizenbaum explains that authentic feelings of empathy are needed from people in these positions. However, there would seem to be conditions where we might prefer to have automated judges and police that have no personal agenda at all.

A Friendly AI is not a tool, but rather a mind that is at least equivalent to a human, and possibly transhuman. Once created, a Friendly AI is independent of its programmers. If an unconscious preconception manages to distort some belief provided by the programmers when the AI is young, the AI will grow up, test the belief, find out that the belief is incorrect, and correct it. A Friendly AI would have full access to its source code and program state, and could thus be more self-aware than an un-augmented human.

Friendliness proponents stress less the danger of a superhuman AI that actively seeks to *harm* humans, but more of an AI that is disastrously indifferent to them. Superintelligent AI may be harmful to humans if steps are not taken to specifically design it to be benevolent. Doing so effectively is the primary goal of Friendly AI. Designing an AI without such *friendliness safeguards*, would be seen as highly immoral, especially if the AI could engage in recursive self-improvement and self-revision potentially leading to a significant power concentration. An AI able to reprogram and improve itself is known as *Seed AI*. Once a seed AI gains a certain degree of intelligence, it could entirely take over the job of programming itself. This could result in an open-ended cycle of intelligence improvement, a Singularity. Seed AI is likely to create a huge power disparity between itself and a statically intelligent human mind. Its ability to enhance itself would very quickly outpace the human ability to exercise any meaningful control over it. A benevolent seed AI could probably do more good for humanity than any other technology, which is why Singularitarians have selected its creation as a humanitarian goal.

Humans are often ill-suited to solving problems in AI, because a human comes with too many built-in inflexible features. Reasoning by analogy with humans is exactly the wrong way to think about Friendly AI. Humans have a complex, intricate architecture. Some of it, from the perspective of a Friendly AI programmer, is worth duplicating, some is decidedly not worth duplicating, and some of it needs to be duplicated, but differently. Assuming that AI automatically possesses negative human functionality leads to expecting the wrong malfunctions; to focusing attention on the wrong problems. Assuming that AIs automatically possess beneficial human functionality means not taking the effort required to deliberately duplicate that functionality.

Anthropomorphism, the attribution of human characteristics or behavior to nonhuman minds, is one of the greatest sources of human error in the analysis of AI psychology, and of Friendly AI in particular. Because human social instincts are emotional instincts, anthropomorphic errors often carry with them a weight of emotional investment, making them unusually hard to dispel. Human analogies are dangerous, both because they assume far too much built-in positive functionality, and because they do not warn against possible negative outcomes resulting from human behaviors, which may not be shared by an AI. The appropriate response to the threat posed by such superintelligence is to attempt to ensure that such intelligent minds specifically feel motivated to not harm other intelligent minds and will deploy their resources towards devising better methods of keeping them from harm. If an AI would be free to murder, injure, or enslave a human being, it would strongly desire not to do so and would only do so if it judged that some vastly greater good to that human or to human beings in general would result. This idea is explored in Asimov's I. Robot stories, via the Zeroth Law: "A robot may not harm humanity, or, by inaction, allow humanity to come to harm".

The Singularity Institute for Artificial Intelligence (SIAI), a nonprofit corporation, has produced *Guidelines* on Friendly AI. The Guidelines do not currently represent an academic consensus or an industry standard. Rather, the SIAI's commitment to Friendly AI is intended as a focal point, around which debate and consensus can grow. The difficulty of creating AI decreases with increasing computing power, but the difficulty of designing Friendly AI does not decrease. Therefore, it is unwise to hold off too long on creating Friendly AI.

One of the more contentious, recent hypotheses in Friendliness theory is the *Coherent Extrapolated Volition model*, also developed by Yudkowsky (2004). He believes that a Friendly AI should initially seek to determine the coherent extrapolated volition of humanity. It should define an objective morality, with which its goals can be set to conform. "Our coherent extrapolated volition is our choices and the result of actions we would collectively take if we knew more, thought faster, were more the people we wished we were, and had grown up closer together. However, it is doubtful that the collective will of humanity will converge to a single coherent set of goals even if we knew more, thought faster, were more the people we wished we were, and had grown up closer together."

Several notable futurists have voiced support for Friendly AI, including author and inventor Raymond Kurzweil, medical life-extension advocate Aubrey de Grey, and World Transhumanist Association co-founder Nick Bostrom of Oxford University. Others, like Ben Goertzel, an AGI researcher, support the basic principles of the Friendly Artificial Intelligence concept, but believe that guaranteed friendliness is not possible. One notable critic of Friendliness theory is the late Hibbard (2002), author of Super-Intelligent Machines, who considers the theory incomplete. Hibbard writes there should be broader political involvement in the design of AI and AI morality, but he also believes that Seed AI could initially only be created by powerful private sector interests. He proposes an AI goal architecture in which human happiness is determined by human behavior. AI should operationalize and try to increase human happiness by applying algorithms that recognize happiness in human facial expressions, voices and body language. Yudkowsky later criticized this proposal by remarking that such an objective would be well satisfied with microscopic smiling mannequins than by making existing humans happier.

5.4 Social Nature of Artificial Intelligence

All of the AI approaches discussed so far essentially view the mind as something associated with a single organism, a single computational system. However, in reality the mind is social—it exists, not in isolated individuals, but in individuals embedded in social and cultural systems.

One approach to incorporate the social aspect of mind is to create individual AGI systems and let them interact with each other. This is an important part of the *Novamente AI project*, which involves a special language for Novamente AI systems to interact with each other (Goetzel 2007).

Another approach is to consider sociality at a more fundamental level, and to create systems from the beginning that are at least as social as they are intelligent. One example of this sort of approach is *Steve Grand's neural-net architecture* as embodied in the *Creatures game*. His neural net based creatures are intended to grow more intelligent by interacting with each other—struggling with each other, learning to outsmart each other, and so forth. *John Holland's classifier systems* are another example of a multi-agent system in which competition and cooperation are both present. The system interacts with an external environment and must react appropriately to the stimuli received from the environment. When the system performs the appropriate actions for a given perception, it receives a reward.

Another important example of social intelligence is research inspired by *social insects*. *Swarm Intelligence* and *Ant Colony Optimization* are popular forms of social intelligence. Swarm Intelligence systems are a new class of biologically inspired tools. These systems are self-organized, relying on direct and indirect communication between agents, and capable of learning and adaptation. These systems are naturally stochastic, relying on multiple interactions and on a random component. They often display highly adaptive behavior in a dynamic environment. Social Intelligence cases show the value of cooperative emergent behavior in an impressive way.

Under *Vladimir Red'ko's self-organizing agent-system approach*, the agents live in a simulated environment in which they can move around, looking for resources, and they can mate. Mating uses the typical genetic operators of uniform crossover and mutation, which leads to the evolution of the agent population. Agents just move around and eat virtual food, accumulating resources to mate. The agents can communicate with each other, and modify their behavior based on their experience. None of the agents individually are all that clever, but they communicate their knowledge about resources, thereby leading to the emergence of adaptive behavior.

5.5 Artificial Intelligence and Robotics

AI has been defined as the part of computer science concerned with designing systems, computer programs to imitate or duplicate human intelligence in computers and robots. A robot is an automatic device that performs functions normally ascribed to humans, or is a machine with the physical form similar to a human or animal. Robotics is the study of the design, construction and use of robots aimed at extending human motor capabilities with machines.

Early technical work in cybernetics gave impetus to the issue of autonomy of robots. The goal was simply to develop a device that can work unattended to arrive at its own conclusions, decisions, and actions. It is important to realize that most work in robotics is *not* devoting any major effort to model something approximating human autonomy.

Typically, autonomy is meant to indicate that there are conditions for which the robot cannot be pre-programmed. This means that various techniques have to be implemented to allow it to adapt, succeed, and survive on its own, "freed" from the intentions of its designers (Pfeifer and Scheier 2001).

AI is realized in software, and robots are manufactured as hardware. The connection between those two is that the control of the robot is a software agent that reads data from the sensors, decides what to do next and then directs the *effectors*, i.e. the means by which robots act in the physical world. One of the most common effectors is the gripper consisting of two fingers which can open and close to pick up and let go of a range of small objects.

The term "robot" can be traced to the Czech author Karel Capek who in 1921 described fabricated workers in a science fiction play called "Rossum's Universal Robots (R.U.R.)". The word "Robot" is derived from the Czech word meaning "forced labor." However, the concept was already present in antiquity. The ancient Greek poet Homer described mechanical helpers. In 1495, Leonardo da Vinci drew plans for a mechanical man. Real robots were only made possible in the 1950s and 1960s with the appearance of transistors and integrated circuits. Following the early instances of robots in plays and science fiction stories, robots started to appear on television shows (an early example is Lost in Space, in which the robot even demonstrated human feelings and emotions) and in Hollywood movies, such as Star Wars. Unimate was the first industrial robot, which worked on a General Motors assembly line in New Jersey, in 1961. The machine undertook the job of transporting die castings from an assembly line and welding these parts on automobile bodies. This was a dangerous task for workers, who could be poisoned by exhaust gas or lose a limb if they were not careful.

To some extent, the field of robotics has followed similar lines as that of AI, attempting to rebound from the overly optimistic predictions of the 1950s and 1960s. While few of the innovations that emerge from robotics research ever appear in the form of robots, their results are widely applied in industrial machines not defined as such.

In spite of significant challenges, there are some good examples of AI-controlled robotic systems. For example, DARPA is in the process of developing an Unmanned Combat Air Vehicle (UCAV) which autonomously performs extremely dangerous and high priority combat missions, which can be revised en route. A distinction can be made between robots working in informational environments, and robots with physical abilities. The former has little need for investment in additional expensive or unreliable robotic hardware, since computer systems and networks provide adequate sensor and effector environments. Physical robots, in contrast, require mechanization of various physical sensory and motor abilities. The challenges involved in providing such an environment are considerable, especially when complete automation is sought.

Robots are also used extensively for exploration in space missions, in the Antarctic, exploring volcanoes, underwater exploration; in medical science robots operate as surgical assistant; in factories robots perform assembly activities; robots are used by bomb squads to locate and dispose of bombs (the Mini-Andros). In 1979 a nuclear accident in the USA caused a leak of radioactive material which led to the production of a special robot to handle this.

However, robots are also designed to perform mundane household tasks, such as grass cutting and nursing, and modern toys which are programmed to do things like talking, walking and dancing.

Robots are used for many of the following reasons. Robots do not get bored with repetitive tasks. Robots never get sick or need time off. Robots can do tasks considered too dangerous or dirty for humans. Robots can operate equipment to much higher precision than humans. Robots may be able to perform tasks that are impossible for humans. Robots may be cheaper over the long term.

Although most robots in use today are designed for specific tasks, the goal is to make universal robots, which are flexible enough to do almost anything a human can do. Robots may be mobile or stationary. Mobile robots move around on legs, tracks or wheels. Stationary robots remain in one place but have arms that move.

Robot teams potentially have applications in a wide range of areas. While individual robots may only have limited capacity, robots working together in groups might be able to perform complex tasks with a functionality that exceeds the sum of their parts. These include military surveillance, mine removal, automated household tasks, large scale laboratory projects and assembly. Robots working in teams allow for solutions in which knowledge, expertise and motor capability may be distributed in time and space.

One potentially far-reaching development involves the development of *cyborg technology*, the applications of which could lead to humans having certain physiological processes aided or controlled by mechanical or electronic devices. In 2009 scientists developed a prosthetic hand, called Smart Hand, which functions like a real one. It allows patients to write, type on a key board, play piano and perform other fine movements. Recent scientific work in neuroscience has allowed people to directly interface their brains, using a number of different technologies. These technologies are often referred to as "brain-computer interfaces" (BCI) which forms a direct connection between a human (or animal) brain with an external device. These connections range from non-invasive technologies that recognize brain signals externally, to invasive technologies that involve surgery and direct electrode implantation. While many of these technologies have the purpose of restoring function to disabled people, others aim to improve upon or augment existing functions.

The most high-profile demonstration in this area is 'robo-rat'. This is a rat with electrodes implanted in the medial forebrain bundle (MFB) and sensorimotor cortex of its brain, developed in 2002 by Sanjiv Talwar and John Chapin at the State University of New York Downstate Medical Center. The rat wears a small electronic backpack containing a radio receiver and electrical stimulator. The rat receives remote stimulation that causes it to feel a sensation in its left or right whiskers, and stimulation in the MFB that is interpreted as a reward or pleasure. This project has been successfully guided by a human controller.

A similar experiment has also been demonstrated by Steve Potter, Professor of Biomedical Engineering at the Georgia Institute of Technology, who has developed a 'rat-controlled robot'. This device results from placing a droplet of solution containing thousands of rat neuron cells onto a silicon chip and then relaying the resulting electrical activity to a robot. The robot then manifests these signals with physical motion, each of its movements a direct result of neurons communicating with neurons. Such examples of merging computer chips with living tissue may seem crude, but scientists describe them as 'momentous'—an event comparable to the first organ transplant or cloned animal. This is because such experiments open up the possibility of using computer technology to supplement human intelligence, rather than to merely replace it.

Robot take-over and machine rights

The possibility of a scenario of AI's overtaking humankind and thus competing with him may generate a call to establish an international commission to monitor and control the development of artificial intelligence systems. A cultural climate of reliance, in which humans allow a position of dependency on AI and robotics to develop with co-evolution, so that human and machine become inextricably intertwined, may be regarded as a possible objective. The strong public reaction to machine takeover appears not to be well-founded in rational arguments, especially is Isaac Asimov's three laws become effective.[2] Nevertheless, the creation of Friendly AI would be a way to address such concerns.

If it becomes possible for humankind to create a truly intelligent machine, a deep issue arises: how will a sentient artificial being be received by humankind and by society? Would it be forced to exist like its machine predecessors, who have effectively been our slaves, or would it enjoy the same rights as the humans who created it, simply because of its intellect? This question touches on religion, politics and law, but to date little serious discussion has been given to the possibility of a new intelligent species and to the rights it might claim.

Socially Intelligent Robots

Humans have always shown a particular curiosity for understanding and simulating nature, and human beings in particular. However, a realistic replication of human activities with smart robots requires recognition of the importance of social intelligence. In the field of human-robot interaction (HRI), the social interaction of robots with people is a necessary part of the research agenda. Previous research on intelligent robots has focused on equipping robots with planning, reasoning, manipulation and other skills necessary to interact with and operate in the non-social environment. However, developing an intelligent robot means developing a socially intelligent robot. This is the research agenda of *developmental robotics*. Dautenhahn (2007) has reviewed research on robots that have social skills and interact with people.

Dautenhahn shows that the notion of social robots and the associated degree of robotic social intelligence is diverse and depends on the particular research

[2] The Three Laws of Robotics are:
Law 1. A robot may not injure a human being, or, through inaction, allow a human being to come to harm;
Law 2. A robot must obey the orders given to it by human beings except where such orders would conflict with the First Law;
Law 3. A robot must protect its own existence as long as such protection does not conflict with the First or Second Law.

emphasis. The first question to be answered is why should robots, where their usefulness and functionality are a primary concern, possess social skills? The answer depends on the specific requirements of a particular domain of application. At one end of the spectrum of the social skill requirements, are those robots, who need only to interact with other robots. At the other end of the spectrum are robots that must interact extensively with humans. Examples include robots that serve as companions in the home for the elderly or assist people with disabilities. They need to possess a wide range of social skills to make them acceptable to humans. Social skills, the development of a robotic etiquette, or *robotiquette*, as a set of heuristics and guidelines on how a robot should behave and communicate in its owner's home are not only desirable but also essential for the acceptance of a robot companion. Without these skills, such robots would fail in their role.

Different paradigms regarding human–robot interaction

Regarding the relationships between humans and robots in HRI, Dautenhahn has distinguished two paradigms: the caretaker paradigm and the assistant/companion paradigm.

The *caretaker paradigm* considers humans as caretakers of robots. The role of the human is to identify and respond to the robot's emotional and social needs. The human needs to keep the robot 'happy'. This implies showing behaviors towards the robot which are characteristic of behavior towards infants or baby animals. This approach is clearly demonstrated in Cynthia Breazeal's (2002) work on *Kismet*, a robotic head with facial features. The robot is meant to be treated as a baby infant or puppy, with exaggerated child-like features satisfying the baby pattern, which appeals to the nurturing instinct in people.

However, it is important to ask whether we really want to bond with computers. Humans are selective regarding how many friends they have. According to Dunbar (2003) there is an evolutionary cognitive limit of 150 on the number of members of our social networks. Thus, if robots are trying to be our friends, and are requiring us to treat them like friends, this might overload our cognitive capacities. Moreover, social interaction and communication with robots is costly, just as with family and friends. Friendship requires emotional, psychological, and physiological investment. Therefore, if humans are expected to interact with robots similarly as with human friends or children, these costs will also occur in HRI. Do we want to make the same investments in robots that we make, for example, in our friends or children? Do we want to worry about how to fulfill our robots' emotional and social needs? Do we get the same 'reward' from an infant robot smiling at us as we would from a child? Is a robot really 'happy' when it smiles? Can mechanical interactions be as rewarding as those with biological organisms? Do we get the same pay-off from HRI, as from human interaction in terms of emotional support, friendship and love? The answers to these questions are not obvious and may be culturally dependent.

The assistant/companion paradigm considers robots as caretakers or assistants of humans. Such a robot has to be considerate, proactive and non-intrusive, to work towards a relationship of trust and confidentiality with the human, to possess good communication skills, to be flexible, to be willing to learn and adapt, and to be competent.

Conclusion

HRI is a young but growing research field. The future will tell whether it will have a long-lasting place in the scientific landscape. According to Dautenhahn, several challenges need to be addressed.

The field of human–computer interaction can provide starting points for the design and analysis of HRI experiments. However, *robots are not people*. In interactions with machines, humans use heuristics derived from human to human interaction. This gives us interesting insights into the social heritage of our intelligence. However, people do not treat machines like human beings (e.g., we immediately replace our broken or inadequate laptop with a new one). Thus, care must be taken when adopting methodologies from social sciences, and apply them unchanged to HRI studies. However, robots are not computers, either. Interacting with physically embodied and socially situated machines is different from interaction via computer interfaces.

HRI is a highly challenging area that requires interdisciplinary collaboration between AI researchers, computer scientists, engineers, psychologists and others. New methods need to be created in order to develop, study and evaluate interactions with a social robot. It may result in social robots that can behave adequately in a human-inhabited social environment, but it also raises many fundamental issues about the nature of social intelligence.

Although the social domain is part of what distinguishes us as human, it is still open as to what social intelligence for robots could or should mean from the perspective of humans. It is unclear whether the social–emotional dimension of human–human interaction can be fulfilled by robots, i.e. whether the inherently mechanical nature of HRIs can allow truly meaningful social exchanges. While it is doubtful that robots can overcome their robotic heritage, it may be more realistic to view them as part of a social environment including human interaction, rather than viewing them as selfish machines.

Examples of Social Robots

Kismet is a robot made in the late 1990s at Massachusetts Institute of Technology by Cynthia Breazeal. The robot's auditory, visual and expressive systems allow it to participate in human social interaction and to demonstrate simulated human emotion and appearance. Kismet contains input devices that give it auditory, visual, and proprioception abilities. Kismet simulates emotion through various facial expressions, vocalizations, and movement. Facial expressions are created through movements of the ears, eyebrows, eyelids, lips, jaw, and head.

To visually perceive the person who interacts with it, Kismet is equipped with four color cameras. A microphone worn by the person is used to process her vocalizations.

The design of Kismet's synthetic nervous system, particularly the perceptual and behavioral aspects, is heavily inspired by the social development of human infants. Kismet is endowed with a substantial amount of infrastructure that enables it to leverage from playful, infant-like interactions, to foster its social development.

The skills and mechanisms allow it to cope with a complex social environment and these skills include feedback to the human it interacts with. It can direct its attention to establish shared reference, and give readable, expressive feedback to the human. It has the ability to recognize expressive feedback such as praise and prohibition, the ability to take turns to reflect the learning episodes, and the ability to regulate interaction to establish a suitable learning environment.

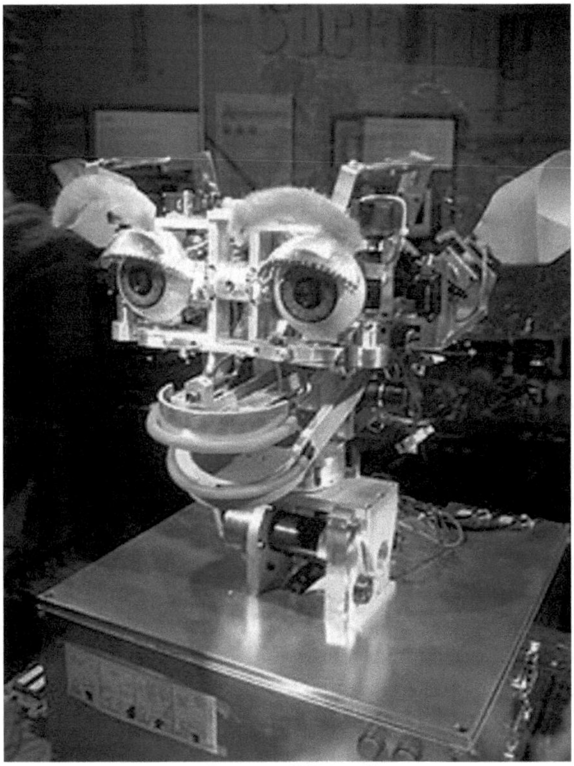

Source: Wikipedia

An example of trials where a mobile robot interacted with children with autism is research project *Aurora* (Autonomous Robotic platform as a Remedial tool for children with Autism) project of the National Autistic Society (NAS) carried out since 1998 in the UK. The aspect of play is a core part of the project, because play is beneficial to children with autism. These children may have difficulty in expressing feelings and thoughts in words. Play gives them chance to express themselves and offers them opportunities to develop the social skills that they lack, in particular turn-taking and imitation.

Robonaut is a humanoid robot under development at NASA's Johnson Space Center to ultimately serve as an astronaut's assistant.

PaReRo is a small mobile household robot under development by NEC corporation.

Health-related applications are also being explored. These include the use of robots as nursemaids to help the elderly, and robotic pets such as Omron's *NeCoRo* that are intended to provide some of the health related benefits of pet ownership. Like most household cats, NeCoRo does not respond to commands or perform tricks. It does what is most important of a cat. It purrs contentedly when stroked and gives cuddly emotional feedback to its owner with feline sounds and movements. NeCoRo can make 48 different cat noises. It can also perk up its ears, squint its eyes, tilt its head, or stretch its legs, to express such feelings as surprise or fatigue.

5.5.1 Can Robots have Emotions?

Science fiction is full of stories of machines that have feelings. Although the gap between science fiction and science fact appears vast, some researchers in artificial intelligence now believe it is only a question of time before it is bridged. The capacity for emotion is often considered to be one of the main differences between humans and machines. This is certainly still true of the machines that exist today. People sometimes get angry with their computers and shout at them as if computers had emotions, but the computers take no notice. They neither recognize human feelings, nor their own feelings.

But the gap between science fiction and science fact is closing. Today's computers and robots still have a long way to go before they acquire a full range of human emotions, but they have already made some progress. In order to make further progress, engineers and computer scientists will have to join forces with psychologists to study robotics and artificial intelligence. The future is in their hands.

The new field of *affective computing* has already made some progress in building primitive emotional machines, and every month brings new advances. However, some critics argue that a machine could never come to have real emotions like ours. At best, they claim, clever programming might allow it to simulate human emotions, but these would just be clever fakes.

In recent years computer scientists have been developing a range of 'animated agent faces'. These are programs that generate images of humanlike faces on the computer's visual display expressing convincing emotions.

The range of emotional expressions available to Kismet is still limited, but these are convincing enough to generate sympathy among the humans who interact with him. Breazeal has invited human parents to play with Kismet on a daily basis. When left alone, Kismet looks sad, but when it detects a human face it smiles, inviting attention.

Does Kismet have emotions? Certainly Kismet has some emotional capacity. Kismet does not display the full range of emotional behavior observed in humans, but the capacity for emotion is not an all-or-nothing thing. There is a whole spectrum of emotional capacities, ranging from the very simple to the very complex. Perhaps Kismet's limited capacity for emotion puts him somewhere near the simple end of the spectrum, but even this is a significant advance over the computers that currently sit on our desks, which by most definitions are devoid of any emotion whatsoever.

As affective computing progresses, it will be possible to build machines with more and more complex emotional capacities. Kismet does not yet have a voice, but in the future Breazeal plans to give him a vocal system which might convey auditory signals of emotion. Today's speech synthesizers speak in an unemotional monotone. In the future, computer scientists will make them sound much more human by modulating nonlinguistic aspects of vocalization like speed, pitch and volume.

Facial expression and vocal intonation are not the only forms of emotional behavior. Emotions may also be inferred from actions. For example, for computers to exhibit the kind of emotional behavior shown by animals when they fear something and turn round and run away, they will have to be able to move around and will have to become *mobots* (mobile robots).

Dozens of mobots have already been developed in laboratories, but most of these are very simple. Some are only the size of a shoe, and all they can do is to find their way around a piece of the floor without bumping into anything. Sensors allow them to detect obstacles such as walls and other mobots. Despite the simplicity of this mechanism, their behavior can seem eerily human. To anybody watching them, the impression that the mobot is actually afraid of collisions is irresistible.

Are these mobots really afraid? Or are spectators guilty of anthropomorphism? The current resistance to attributing emotions to machines is simply due to the fact that even the most advanced machines today are still very primitive. As machines come to resemble humans more, the question about whether or not the machines have 'real' emotions or just 'fake' ones will become less meaningful. Some experts estimate that we will be able to build machines with complex emotions like ours within fifty years. But is this a good idea? What is the point of building emotional machines? Would emotions just get in the way of good computing, or even worse, cause computers to turn against humans?

Reasons to Give Computers Emotions

Giving computers emotions could be very useful for a variety of reasons. First, it would be much easier and more enjoyable to interact with an emotional computer than with today's unemotional machines. If, by scanning your facial expression, the computer detects that you are in a bad mood, the emotionally-aware desktop PC might tell you a joke, or suggest that you read a particularly nice email first. If you resent such attempts to cheer you up, the computer might ignore you until you had calmed down or had a coffee. Hence, it might be much more productive to work with a computer that was emotionally intelligent in this way than with today's dumb machines.

This is not just a flight of fancy. Computers are already capable of recognizing some emotions. A computer is able to recognize facial expressions of six basic emotions. Paired with volunteers who pretended to feel one of these emotions, the computer recognized the emotion correctly 98 % of the cases. This is better than the accuracy rate achieved by most humans on the same task! If computers are already better than us at recognizing some emotions, it is surely not long before they will acquire similarly advanced capacities for expressing emotions, and perhaps even for feeling them. In the future, it may be humans who are seen by computers as emotionally awkward, not vice versa.

Many other possible applications for emotional computers have been proposed, including the following:

- Artificial interviewers that train humans on how to do well in job interviews by giving feedback on human body language.
- Affective voice synthesizers that allow people with speech problems not just to speak, but to speak in genuinely emotional ways.
- Frustration monitors that allow manufacturers to evaluate how easy their products are to use.
- Wearable computers ('intelligent clothing') that give feedback on human emotional states so that they can tell when humans are getting stressed and need a break.

All of these potential applications for emotional machines are resolutely utilitarian, but probably many or most emotional machines in the future will be built not for any practical purpose, but purely for entertainment. Instead of for spacecraft and intelligent clothing, they will be for toys and video games. The constant demand for better games means that game software is continually improving. It might well be that the first genuinely emotional computers are game consoles.

Entertainment software with proto-emotional capacities is already available in the form of virtual pets, which live in personal computers. Many kids now keep dogs and cats as screen-pets, and more recently a virtual baby has been launched. A program called Sims allows you to design your own people. Soon they may take on a life of their own, which can be fascinating to watch. As characters, the Sims are eerily human in their range of emotional behavior: they get angry, become depressed, and even fall in love.

There are also little furry robots, called *Furbies*, which[3] fall asleep when tired, and make plaintive cries when neglected for too long. There are also robotic dogs and cats that run around your living room without ever making a mess. There is even a baby doll with a silicon brain and a latex face that expresses distress when it needs feeding.

All of these creatures are Virtual. They live inside the computer, and their only body is a picture on a screen. However, the first computerized creatures with real bodies are also now coming onto the toy market, and they too have proto-emotional

[3] In the future, when robots really look and act like humans they might be referred to as "who", rather than "which".

capacities. Most people respond to these artificial life forms with natural sympathy. They enjoy playing with them, as they would with a real kitten or baby.

Is it possible to design computers with emotions?

It is now possible to design a relatively simple machine that can monitor and control both things in the outside world, and things inside itself. If the wiring is done right, even a simple robot can be said to have states that are analogues of some human emotions. But it does not necessarily have a complex emotional life. To have that requires making machines that interact with people in more natural ways. However, it may be argued that because a machine cannot physically feel (itself an assumption up for debate), it would be contradictory to suggest that it would be capable of having emotions.

Should computers with emotions be designed?

If a machine is to survive, it needs something like emotions to help it respond rapidly and appropriately to changes in its environment. There is definitely a need to make complex, flexible robots easy to interact with. They must be understandable to us, and vice versa. Therefore, it would be useful if they could show, recognize, and understand emotions.

How would the computer react to or measure human emotions if it was to have emotions itself?

Much ongoing work is about getting computers to recognize human emotions from information extracted from skin galvanometry (measuring levels of sweating), tone of voice, facial expression, and so on. This research is interesting, but does not get at the core of human emotions. A computer might be able to tell that someone is happy, but it could not (easily) tell what she is happy about. To get this kind of information, computers need to able to tell what people are looking at, when they feel an emotion, and what they mean when they talk about the world. Much of our conversation and body language reveals how we feel about things, directly or indirectly and to tap into this, computers will need to be able to understand human communication better.

Could a computer with emotions have a personality?

This seems very likely. First, most people experience emotions when they interact with the world and with each other. These emotions vary from person to person. That is a feature of personality. If a computer has emotions at all, it will automatically project a personality. Secondly, in building emotional robots, it makes sense to make them different from one another, rather than giving them all identical personalities.

Does the irrational nature of emotion not conflict with the fundamental way in which programs and computers are designed?

A distinction commonly made is that between emotion and reason. This separation has gone too far, and it has been convincingly argued that much reasoning involves emotion (Damasio 1995). In terms of programming, what matters is whether functional relationships can be worked out between cognitive states (like beliefs about the world) and affective states (like strong, positive preferences for particular experiences). If there are regular functional relationships, which seems likely, the problem can be tackled.

What is it like to be a conscious computer?

The subjective nature of consciousness means that it is impossible to know if a computer is *experiencing* emotions. Therefore, there is no concept of what it is like *to be a conscious computer.* In accordance with the Turing-esque definition, "if it looks like a duck and quacks like a duck, then it is a duck", and if robots can be made to behave in complex ways similar to people, then there is no reason to deny them emotional feelings, or conscious states.

5.6 Whole Brain Emulation

Whole Brain Emulation (WBE) is the transfer of a mind, the mental structure and consciousness of a person, from a biological brain to an external carrier, such as a computer. The term emulation originates in computer science, where it denotes closely copying the function of a program or computer hardware by having its functions simulated by another program. While a *simulation* imitates the outward results, *emulation* mimics the internal causal dynamics (at some suitable level of description). The emulation is regarded as successful if the emulated system produces the same outward behavior and results as the original (possibly with a difference in speed).

It can be said that a *brain emulator* is software that models the states and functional dynamics of a brain at a relatively fine-grained level of detail. In particular, a *mind emulation* is a brain emulator that is detailed and correct enough to produce the phenomenological (subjective experience) effects of a mind.

In the brain, every molecule is a powerful computer and the structure and function of trillions upon trillions of molecules, as well as all the rules that govern how they interact, must be simulated. Although computers that are trillions of times bigger and faster than anything existing today are needed, a detailed functional artificial human brain can be built in principle. Substantial mainstream research is being done in the development of faster super computers, virtual reality, brain–computer interfaces, animal brain mapping, and simulation. Super computers are expected to reach sufficient capacity for whole human brain emulation within a few years.

The established neuroscientific consensus is that the human mind is largely a property of the information processing of the neural network, which can be emulated. The human brain contains about 100 billion nerve cells called neurons, each individually linked to other neurons along neural pathways. Signals at the terminus of axons, are transmitted across synapses to the next neurons on the pathway, by chemical, electrical or mechanical means, depending on the type of neuron. Neuroscientists assume that important functions performed by the mind, such as learning, memory, and consciousness, are due to purely physical and electrochemical processes in the brain. Many neural pathways for specific functions of the brain have been already documented, with the relevant sensory, association, and motor areas identified.

The word emulation describes the aim of achieving as close a functional match as possible, so that the mind is altered as little as possible in the transfer keeping the individuality as intact as possible. WBE is not the "creation" of a new mind. Since so much of human thinking is directed towards physical needs and desires and a person's personality and skills reside in the brain, a re-instantiated mind needs a body. A successful emulation *need not predict all details of the original behavior* of the emulated system; it need only replicate *computationally relevant functionality* at the desired level of emulation.

Mind uploading (another term for WBE) is consistent with the view of modern neuroscience and cognitive theory that consciousness does not require some mysterious, immaterial, energizing force, but is contained in the physical interactions of a brain and its structure, and can thus be quantified and described. In cases where the subject's consciousness is transferred to a memory device, the result is an artificial intelligence. If a memory device is lodged in an artificial body, the result is a "thinking" robot. A very important question is whether or not your uploaded human brain is really you. An important element in uploading will be the gradual transfer of intelligence, personality, and skills, to the nonbiological portion of human intelligence.

According to Kurzweil, in the 2020s, nanobots will augment our brain with nonbiological intelligence, starting with routine functions of sensory processing and memory, moving on to skill formation, pattern recognition, and logical analysis. By the 2030s, the nonbiological portion of our intelligence will predominate, because biological intelligence is essentially fixed in its capacity. By the 2040s, the nonbiological portion will be billions of times more capable. Gradually we would have effectively uploaded ourselves, never quite noticing the transfer. There would be no "Old Me" and no "New Me", but just an increasingly capable "Me". This gradual but inexorable progression to vastly superior nonbiological thinking would profoundly transform human civilization.

The technologically simplest approach is destructive scanning or serial sectioning in which the brain is destructively disassembled during the emulation process. This could be applied immediately after death or on cryogenically preserved brain tissue. *Serial sectioning* involves freezing a brain, slicing it up using a laser or a diamond knife, examining the slices under a microscope, and reconstructing the neurons, synapses and most of the major brain components that are deemed functionally imperative, in an artificial brain. There is a need for methods of physically handling and storing pieces of tissue. Since most scanning methods cannot image large volumes, the brains will have to be sectioned into manageable pieces with less tolerance for damage.

Nanotechnology may prove useful in mapping out the brain. The brain will be infused with nanoparticles which will map out the brain's physical structure and record chemical interactions. While in deep sleep, the nanomachines circulate throughout the brain, and replace existing neurons with electronic equivalents. In this case, the person will still be living and interacting with his environment as if nothing has happened and he is clearly alive. Hence, the basic idea is to take a particular brain, scan its structure in detail, and construct a software model of it that is so faithful to the original that, when run on appropriate hardware, it will behave in essentially the same way as the original brain.

Non-destructive scanning of living brains appears to be more difficult than the "slice-and-dice" approach. Nanomedical techniques may possibly enable non-destructive scanning by use of *invasive* measurement devices. Nanobots could replace damaged brain cells with artificial ones, making way for a step by step or gradual transition to an artificial brain. This method is similar to another proposal termed *cyborging*, which also maps the brain and its functions, and replaces each component with an artificial one. This may be done systematically until the entire brain has been replaced by artificial components.

A common doubt expressed about the possibility of simulating even simple neural systems is that they are analog rather than digital. The doubt is based on the qualitative difference between continuous and discrete variables. If computations in the brain make use of the full power of continuous variables the brain may be able to achieve "hyper-computation". Brains are made of imperfect structures which are, in turn, made of discrete atoms obeying quantum mechanical rules, which force them into discrete energy states. Nevertheless, it is questionable whether quantum computing is required for WBE. Part of Sect. 5.6 is devoted to this issue.

At present, emulating the human brain is not much more than a futuristic speculation. We do not understand enough about the brain to make detailed simulations of brain functions. At present much research is ongoing about the modeling of complex neural structures. This has resulted only in neural models of different parts of a mind, which may be considered as building blocks for a compete AGI design. Intelligent nanobots (blood cell-sized computerized robots) would be sent into the human brain through the capillaries to intimately interact with biological neurons. IBM is now building a detailed simulation of a substantial portion of the cerebral cortex in the brain.

An organization called the *Brain Preservation Foundation* was founded in 2010 and is offering a Brain Preservation Technology prize, to promote exploration of brain preservation technology in service of humanity. The Prize, currently \$106,000, will be awarded in two parts, 25 % to the first international team to preserve a whole mouse brain, and 75 % to the first team to preserve a whole large animal brain in a manner that could also be adopted for humans, in a hospital or hospice setting, immediately upon clinical death. Ultimately the goal of this prize is to generate a whole brain map which may be used in support of separate efforts to upload and possibly 'reboot' a mind in virtual space.

5.6.1 What are the Potential Benefits of WBE?

Immortality/Backup

In theory, if the information and processes of the mind can be disassociated from the biological body, they are no longer tied to the individual limits and lifespan of that body. Information within a brain could be partly or wholly copied or transferred to one or more other substrates (including digital storage or another brain), thereby reducing or eliminating mortality risk.

Speed-Up

A computer-based intelligence such as an upload could potentially *think much faster* than a human even if it were no more intelligent. Human neurons exchange electrochemical signals with a maximum speed of about 150 m per second, whereas the speed of light is about 300 million meters per second, about two million times faster. Also, neurons can generate a maximum of about 200 to 1000 action potentials or "firings" per second, whereas the number of signals per second in modern computer chips is about 2 GHz (about ten million times greater), and expected to increase rapidly. Eliezer Yudkowsky of the Singularity Institute for Artificial Intelligence has calculated a theoretical upper bound for the speed of a future artificial neural network. It could, in theory, run about 1 million times faster than a real brain, experiencing about a year of subjective time in only 31 s of real time. That requires an enormously powerful computer or artificial neural network in comparison with today's super-computers. The processing demands are likely to be immense, due to the large number of neurons in the human brain, along with the considerable complexity of each neuron.

Multiple/Parallel Existence

A concept explored in science fiction is the idea of more than one running copy of a human mind existing at once. Such copies could potentially allow an "individual" to experience many things at once, and later integrate the experiences of all copies into a central mentality at some point in the future. This effectively allows a single sentient being to be at many places at once and do many things at once. Such partial and complete copies of a sentient being raise interesting questions regarding identity and individuality.

Copying Versus Moving

Another issue with brain uploading is what the difference would be between a replica and the original and whether an uploaded mind is really the "same" sentience. This is the subject of the *Swampman thought experiment.*[4] This issue is especially complex if the original remains essentially unchanged by the uploading procedure, thereby resulting in an obvious copy which could potentially have rights separate from the unaltered, obvious original.

Most projected brain scanning technologies may necessarily be destructive so that the original brain would not survive the brain scanning procedure. But if it can be kept intact, the computer-based consciousness could be a copy of the still-living biological person. Since a brain emulation can be started, paused, backed-up and rerun from a saved backup state at any time, the emulated mind would forget everything that has happened after the instant of backup. In that case an older version of a simulated mind may meet a younger version and share experiences with it.

WBE requires significant computer power and storage for image processing and interpretation during the scanning process, and to hold and run the resulting emulation. However, it does appear feasible within the foreseeable future to store the full connectivity of all neurons in the brain within the working memory of a large computing system. Achieving the performance needed for real-time emulation appears to be a more serious computational problem, but full human brain emulations should be possible before mid-century. Animal models of simple mammals would be possible one to two decades before this.

There do not appear to exist any obstacles to attempting to emulate an invertebrate organism today, but the networks that make up the brains of even modestly complex organisms, are still not fully known. Obtaining detailed anatomical information of a small brain appears entirely feasible and useful to neuroscience, and would be a critical first step towards WBE.

It seems that the need for raw computing power for real-time simulation and funding for building large-scale automated scanning/processing facilities, are the factors most likely delay the advent of WBE.

---

[4] Swampman is the subject of a thought experiment introduced by Donald Davidson, in his 1987 paper "Knowing One's Own Mind". The experiment runs as follows: Suppose Davidson goes hiking in the swamp and is struck and killed during a storm by a lightning bolt. At the same time, nearby in the swamp another lightning bolt spontaneously rearranges a bunch of molecules such that, entirely by coincidence, they take on exactly the same form that Davidson's body had at the moment of his untimely death. This copy, whom Davidson terms 'Swampman', has a brain which is identical to that which Davidson had, and will thus, presumably, behave exactly as Davidson would have. He will walk out of the swamp, return to Davidson's office and write the same essays he would have written; he will interact like an amicable person with all of Davidson's friends and family, and so forth. But Davidson holds that there would nevertheless be a difference, though no one would notice it. Swampman will appear to recognize Davidson's friends, but actually he will not recognize them, as he has never seen them before.

5.6.2 Brain Computer Interface

Mind uploading can be seen as a migration process of the core mental functions, which are transferred from a human brain to an artificial environment. This process might be performed with a brain–computer interface, brain transplant or prosthesis.

A brain–computer interface (BCI) or a brain–machine interface (BMI), is a direct pathway of communication between the brain and an external device. BCIs are often aimed at assisting, augmenting, or repairing human cognitive or sensory-motor functions. Research on BCIs began in the 1970s at the University of California Los Angeles (UCLA) under a grant from the National Science Foundation, followed by a contract from DARPA. The field of BCI research and development has since focused primarily on neuroprosthetic applications that aim at restoring damaged hearing, sight and movement. Thanks to the remarkable plasticity of the cerebral cortex, signals from implanted prostheses can, after adaptation, be handled by the brain like natural sensor or effector channels. Following years of animal experimentation, the first neuroprosthetic devices implanted in humans appeared in the mid-nineties.

Neuroprosthetics is an area of neuroscience concerned with neural prostheses—using artificial devices to replace the function of impaired nervous systems or sensory organs. The most widely used neuroprosthetic device is the cochlear implant, which, as of 2006, has been implanted in approximately 100,000 people worldwide. There are several neuroprosthetic devices that aim to restore vision, including retinal implants.

The differences between BCIs and neuroprosthetics are mostly in the ways the terms are used: neuroprosthetics typically connect the nervous system to a device, whereas BCIs usually connect the brain (or nervous system) with a computer system. Practical neuroprosthetics can be linked to any part of the nervous system—for example, peripheral nerves—while the term "BCI" usually designates a narrower class of systems which interface with the central nervous system. Sometimes the terms are used interchangeably. Neuroprosthetics and BCIs seek to achieve the same aims, such as restoring sight, hearing, movement, ability to communicate, and even cognitive function. Both use similar experimental methods and surgical techniques.

A distinction can be made between invasive and non-invasive BCIs. Invasive BCI research aims at repairing damaged sight and providing new functionality to persons with paralysis. Invasive BCIs are implanted directly into the grey matter of the brain during neurosurgery. Since they rest in the grey matter, invasive devices produce the highest quality signals among BCI devices. However, they are prone to create scar-tissue build-up, causing the signal to become weaker or even lost, as the body reacts to a foreign object in the brain.

Besides invasive experiments, there have also been experiments in humans using non-invasive, neuroimaging technologies as interfaces. Signals recorded in this way have been used to power muscle implants and restore partial movement in an experimental volunteer. Although they are easy to wear, non-invasive implants produce poor signal resolution because the skull dampens signals, dispersing and blurring the electromagnetic waves created by the neurons. Although the waves can still be detected, it is more difficult to determine the area of the brain that is exhibiting activation.

Electroencephalography (EEG) is the most studied potential non-invasive interface, due mainly to its fine temporal resolution, ease of use, portability and low set-up cost. Besides the technology's susceptibility to noise, another substantial barrier to using EEG as a brain–computer interface is the extensive training required before users can work with the technology.

MEG (Magnetoencephalography) and MRI (Magnetic resonance imaging)

MEG and functional MRI (fMRI) have both been used successfully as non-invasive BCIs. While also imperfect, fMRI is better suited to identifying the location of neurons that are firing. fMRI measurements of haemodynamic responses in real time have been used to control robot arms with a seven second delay between thought and movement.

BCI Based Toys

A number of companies have scaled back medical grade EEG technology to create inexpensive BCIs for toys and gaming devices. Some of these toys have been extremely commercially successful. These include NeuroSky and Mattel MindFlex.

5.6.3 Preparing for Mind Uploading

Assuming mind uploading will take place in an immediate as opposed to gradual form, waking up may presumably occur in one of two kinds of bodies. This may happen in a human body that wasn't yours previously (either because it is the body of a person who suffered brain death or because a brainless body was genetically grown for you). It also may involve waking up in some sort of computer environment, like a robot. Waking up in another human body is not likely and is not really what mind uploading is all about anyway. In the second situation robots of the future will be free to be supple, graceful, warm, and articulate.

Waking will happen in a body that was not yours previously. This can be both physically and mentally challenging. Preparation does not consist of physical preparation because the old body is not needed anymore, but mental preparation is necessary. You will appear different to other people who know you because you will have different physical abilities and the robotic replacement body will likely surpass the original body in most aspects.

Uploading would cause a dramatic shift in human society. Uploaded minds will be on a fast track to accelerated evolution and growth while "leftover" humans will probably seem pretty dull by comparison. Preparation will depend on whether there is a short or long period of transition from the first upload to a society of primarily cybernetic humans.

If mind uploading induces a sudden alteration of society, the entire revolution will probably be over fairly quickly. Initially, uploading would be expensive but the costs would be expected to decline over time. The rich would get it first and the rest get it later. Aside from the financial cost, a lot of people will not accept uploaded humans as a matter of principle. Religious people may declare uploaded people dead and soulless and their very consciousness may be denied. It is unclear how religious authorities would pronounce on the matter.

For late uploaders, preparation is not something to worry about because uploading would be occurring en-masse with well-organized forms of training and possibilities to buy an uploading kit. However, a gradual revolution would seem unlikely in the case of a fast uploading procedure, though it might be more likely if the uploading process itself is gradual, by way of cybernetic implants or slow brain augmentation. This method of uploading may be more realistic than fast uploading. Uploading may be something that can be done so quietly that other people do not notice each stage. If the uploading procedure occurs near the end of this quiet revolution, then people will have gradually come to accept mind uploading. What about *physical preparation*? Depending on the method of mind uploading, your original body could be totally unaffected or may have to be destroyed. The best you can do before mind uploading becomes reality is to keep your body healthy. There are not one, but two very good reasons to adopt a long-term attitude toward your health in anticipation of new technologies.

The first reason is that mind uploading provides you with a dramatically extended lifespan. The uploaded mind may only be as good as the mind it is uploaded from. Thus, research into Parkinson's, Alzheimer's, Schizophrenia, Depression, and other brain diseases is especially valuable. Such research will ensure the health of our brains long enough to get to the forthcoming uploading revolution, but it will also accelerate brain research in general and thus bring the day of feasible mind-uploading closer to the present.

The second reason to care about your health is to avoid death until mind uploading becomes possible. As old-age sets in, a brain and mind that are kept busy and stimulated will remain more adaptive and healthy. Keep yourself occupied. Find things you are excited about and embrace them. Maintaining your vitality will be absolutely essential to make it to the day when mind uploading will be available, and to have a mind fit to upload.

5.6.4 The Costs and Benefits of Mind Uploading

Uploading requires not only a complete understanding of neuroscience, but also perfect knowledge of how to convert every relevant aspect of the brain's functioning into electronic computation. According to Agar (2011) mind-uploading is prudentially irrational. Success in mind uploading relies on the soundness of the program of Strong AI—the view that it may someday be possible to build a computer that is capable of thought. If Strong AI is a correct view, uploaded humans can enjoy the benefits of enhanced cognition unavailable to those who retain their biological brains. Conversely, if Strong AI is a false view, then no computer could ever serve as a receptacle for a human mind, and mind-uploading would inevitably fail.

According to Nicolas Agar the probability of strong AI being true is somewhat less than 1, and he therefore concludes that mind-uploading is *prudentially irrational.*

It may be argued that even those who are convinced by the possibility of mind uploading should also take into account that there is a non-negligible chance that they are mistaken, and that mind-uploading is fatal. There certainly is a non-zero probability that any manner of "brain emulation" could result in death.

An important question is whether there is reason for thinking that the probability of death-by-uploading is sufficiently high to justify refusal. Mind-uploading might be worthwhile if the risks of death are small and the potential gains are great.

There may be people who would be undeterred by the risk of death (or an equivalent loss) from failed mind-uploading. A person about to expire from a terminal illness can choose between certain death from disease and a merely possible death from uploading failure.

If the gerontologist *Aubrey de Grey* is right about the near future of our species, we could soon become ageless, immunized against cancer, heart failure, or any of the other diseases that might incline us to disregard caution about uploading. He claims that there is a good chance that people alive today will achieve millennial life spans. They will do this by systematically fixing up their brains and bodies, without recourse to uploading. *Longevity Escape Velocity is likely to arrive sooner than uploading*.

If mind-uploading is perfected in advance of achieving longevity escape velocity, it is possible that candidates for uploading which have been diagnosed with terminal cancer have nothing or very little to lose from uploading. Then, uploading could be prudentially rational for them. Those who are not terminally ill may direct their hopes and expectations toward lower-risk methods of life extension and quality of life improvement.

The citizens of societies with mind-uploading technologies may find the risk of death or the loss of their conscious minds from failed mind-uploading acceptable if counterbalanced by very considerable benefits from successful mind-uploading. If a mind can be uploaded in the near future, the value of protecting one's brain from injury or damage becomes much higher than for other organs, which will lose relative value with the advent of uploading.

John Pavius has provided 6 reasons why he feels will be impossible to upload the human mind into a computer.

1. Overload of the platform onto which the uploading is done is likely. This is a common problem that the most advanced computer scientists are struggling with. In principle, backups of uploaded minds can be made. But is the "backup" really you, or is it just a clone of you that takes your place now that the "real" you is lost?
2. The storage media won't last five years, Much Less Forever. Digital storage media may collapse alarmingly fast when used continuously by millions of people "living" on them. Without frequent physical backups, refreshes, and format updates, precious data will quickly be rendered unreadable or inaccessible.
3. Insane energy demand. The human brain only needs 20 w to run the application called "You", but with almost 7 billion humans, the earth's ability to host all

humans will be straining. This requires the invention of a new energy technology, such as fusion reactors or a Dyson sphere,

4. Lack of processing power. Adding up the brain's billions of neurons and trillions of synapses gives a "total processing power" of about 10 quadrillion calculations per second, or 10 petaflops. However, neuroscientists are still uncovering all the ways that the little wires in our heads encode information and this requires an enormous amount extra computational energy exceeding that 10-quadrillion figure by several orders of magnitude.
5. Minds do not work without bodies. What makes you "You" is not just the information content of your memories and conscious mind—it's the whole dynamic physical makeup and history of your body. In fact, barely anything is known about what specific jobs all of the brain's structures actually evolved for, but an emerging consensus is that the brain's main job is simply to keep track of what various parts of your body are doing (or should be doing). Meanwhile, the special human conscious self is an evolutionary latecomer that became a feature under the delusion that it is in charge but really just along for the ride.

This means that, because the human mind is merely a component of the body, it is not possible to separate the two—at least, not without losing everything you know and experience as "yourself". Experiments have shown that people's personalities can change if they are embodied just slightly differently via virtual reality. Studies on amputees have shown that removing body parts affects visual perception. Even simple abstract notions (like "past" and "future", "like" and "dislike," even "you" and "I") boil down to physical sensations of the body in space.

6. Who Gets Uploaded? Unless there is a way to upload all of humanity simultaneously, there will be fighting over who goes first, how long it takes, what it costs, who pays, and how long they get to stay there.

5.6.5 Conclusions

The brain might be physically duplicated with brain-scanning, but to upload a particular person's personality, neural processes must be simulated at the level of individual neurons. Virtual worlds seem to provide an ideal environment for the creation and maturation of powerful AGI systems. Creating virtual neurons, synapses and activations is another way to let the brain guide AGI. Humans would be uploaded into virtual bodies, and live in virtual worlds with a high level of integration between AGIs and human society. Social interaction in virtual worlds is a domain that requires general intelligence on the human level, and is not amenable to narrow AI techniques. By the time of the Singularity, humans may essentially be inseparable from the AGI-incorporating technological substrate they have created. Right now many people already consider themselves inseparable from their cell-phones and the Internet. AGIs involved in the *metaverse*, i.e. the universe of virtual worlds, become progressively more and more intelligent due to their integration in the social network of human beings interacting with them.

Eventually, AGI's will have many significant advantages over biological intelligences. The ability to modify their own underlying structures and dynamics, will give AGI an ability for self-improvement that vastly exceeds that possessed by humans. AGI designs based too closely on the human brain may not be able to exploit the unique advantages available to digital intelligences. Approaches that provide greater efficiency on available computer hardware seem sensible at the present time.

5.7 Creating Artificial Live: ALife

If simulating the brain molecule by molecule is not ambitious enough, there is another possible approach to AGI that is even more ambitious: simulation of the sort of evolutionary processes that gave rise to the human brain in the first place. Although a super- computer cannot yet simulate the origin of life on Earth molecule by molecule, it is possible to emulate the type of process where by life emerges: cells from organic molecules, multi-cellular organisms from unicellular ones. This kind of research falls into the domain of artificial life (Alife) rather than AI proper. The fields of AI and artificial life overlap, as living and flourishing in a changing and uncertain environment seem to require at least a rudimentary form of intelligence.

Artificial life attempts to understand the essential general properties of living systems by synthesizing life-like behavior in software, hardware and biochemicals. The rules governing the elements of complex systems, which have to be reshaped over time by some process of adaptation or learning, are the main focus of artificial life.

The phrase 'artificial life' was coined by Langton (1995), who envisioned a study of life *as it could* be in any possible setting. Artificial life owes its deepest intellectual roots to John von Neumann and Norbert Wiener. Von Neumann tried to understand the fundamental properties of living systems, especially self-reproduction and the evolution of complex adaptive structures, by constructing simple formal systems that exhibited those properties. Wiener started applying information theory and the analysis of self-regulatory processes to the study of living systems. The constructive and abstract methodology of cellular automata still typifies much of artificial life, as does the abstract and material-independent methodology of information theory.

There is an important difference between the modeling strategies of traditional AI and artificial life. Most traditional AI models are *top–down-specified serial systems* involving a centralized controller who makes decisions, which have the potential to affect directly any aspect of the whole system. ALife's models are *bottom-up-specified*, parallel systems of simple agents, interacting locally. They are repeatedly iterated and the resulting global behavior is observed. Such lower-level models are sometimes said to be 'agent-based' or 'individual-based.' The whole system's behavior is represented only indirectly, and arises out of the interactions of constituent parts, both with each other and with their physical and social environment.

Artificial life (also known as 'ALife') is an interdisciplinary study of life and life-like processes that involves synthesizing that behavior in artificial systems.

Our technological capabilities have brought us to the point where we are on the verge of creating "living" artifacts. Artificial life is an alternative life-form: life made by Man rather than by Nature, using artificial rather than living cells. Artificial Life expands our sense of what is possible, and it provides a constructive way to explore it. Although artificial life is fundamentally directed towards both the origins of biology and its future, the scope and complexity of its subject require interdisciplinary cooperation and collaboration.

Artificial Life aims to investigate the possibility of discovering lifelike behavior in unfamiliar settings, to create new and unfamiliar forms of life, and to develop a coherent theory of life in all its manifestations. It may help individuals to use new technologies for extending life and creating new forms of life, using drugs, prosthetics, the Internet, evolvable hardware, and proliferating robots. Artificial life is foremost a scientific, rather than an engineering, endeavor. Given how ignorant we still are about the emergence and evolution of living systems, artificial life should emphasize understanding first and applications second.

Artificial Life highlights the question of whether artificial constructions, especially the purely digital systems existing in computers, could ever literally be alive. The answer to this question requires agreement about the nature of life. However such agreement should not be expected until we have experienced a much broader range of possibilities. Artificial life's self-conscious aim to discern the essence of life encourages a liberal experimentation with novel life-like organisms and processes. Thus, artificial life fosters a broad perspective on life.

While biology research is essentially *analytic*, attempting to break down complex phenomena into their basic components, Alife is *synthetic*, trying to construct phenomena from their elemental units putting together systems that behave like living organisms. Biology studies phenomena associated with life on earth, that is, *life-as-we-know-it*, while Alife studies the large domain of biological possible life, that is, *life-as-it-could-be*.

Artificial life amounts to the practice of "*synthetic biology*," and the attempt to recreate biological phenomena in alternative media would result in not only better theoretical understanding of the phenomena under study, but also in practical applications of biological principles in industry and technology.

In the long run, artificial life can contribute to the development of practical adaptive systems in many fields of application, such as software development and management, design and manufacture of robots, including distributed swarms of autonomous agents, automated trading in financial markets, pharmaceutical design, ecological sustainability, and extraterrestrial exploration.

Because intelligence is a property of living systems, AI might be seen as a subfield of A-Life. Artificial life is interested in understanding the properties of living organisms, so that they can build artificial systems that exhibit these properties for useful purposes. While AI researchers are interested mostly in perception, cognition and generation of action, Alife focuses on evolution, reproduction, morphogenesis and metabolism. AI attempts to replicate human intelligence, whereas Alife attempts to emulate the behavior of organic life systems. Alife may or may not be intelligent.

Evolution is central to Alife and it offers the possibility of adaptation to a dynamic environment. When an unforeseen event occurs, the system can evolve, analogously to nature. An evolutionary method is advantageous not only in solving problems, but also in offering better adaptability. The evolution of life has shown a remarkable growth in complexity. Simple *prokaryotic one-celled* life has led to more complex *eukaryotic single-celled life*,[5] which then led to multicellular life, then to large-bodied vertebrate creatures with sophisticated sensory processing capacities, and ultimately to highly intelligent creatures that use language and develop sophisticated technology. This illustration of evolution's creative potential leads to a deep question. Does evolution have an inherent tendency to create greater and greater adaptive complexity, or is the complexity of life as we know it just a contingent and accidental by-product of evolution?

Much effort in artificial life is directed towards creating a system that shows how this kind of open-ended evolutionary progress is possible, even in principle. Although some forms of life remain evolutionary stable for millions of years (e.g., sharks), the apparently open-ended growth in complexity of the most complex organisms is intriguing and puzzling. Open-ended adaptability is a hallmark of life, at least when considered on an evolutionary time scale. The ability to cope with a complex, dynamic, unpredictable environment is a defining feature of cognitive and intelligent systems. This implies that there is a fundamental similarity in the key mechanisms behind both living and cognitive systems, and the future of both AI and artificial life hinges on bridging the gap between non-living and living matter. Artificial and natural evolving systems are qualitatively different classes of evolutionary dynamics, and no known artificial system generates the kind of evolutionary dynamics exhibited by the biosphere. Some key insights are still missing about the mechanisms whereby evolution continually creates new kinds of environments that elicit new kinds of adaptations.

Evolvability, the capacity of evolution to create new adaptations, depends on a system's ability to produce adaptive *phenotypic* variation, and this hinges on both the extent to which phenotype space contains adaptive variation and the ability of evolutionary search to find it. For evolutionary search to explore a suitable variety of viable evolutionary pathways, genetic operators must generate enough evolutionary novelty. At the same time, evolutionary memory is needed to retain incremental improvements discovered over time. Evolvability requires successfully and flexibly balancing these competing demands for novelty and memory; this is known as the 'explore–exploit' *trade-off* in the machine learning literature.

Genetic algorithms are currently the most prominent and widely-used computational models of evolution in artificial life systems. A genetic algorithm is a machine-learning technique loosely modeled on biological evolution; it views learning as a matter of competition among candidate problem solutions. Potential

[5] Prokaryotes are organisms that lack a cell nucleus or a membrane-bound kernel. Everything is openly accessible within the cell so that the DNA is not collected together in the area the membrane encloses. Eukaryotes are organisms whose cells contain complex structures enclosed within membranes which contain their DNA.

solutions are encoded in an artificial chromosome, and an initial population of candidate solutions is created randomly. The quality or 'fitness' of each solution is calculated by application of a 'fitness function'. For example, if the problem is to find the shortest route between two cities and a candidate solution is a specific itinerary, then the fitness function might be the reciprocal of the sum of the distances of each segment in the itinerary, so that shorter-distance routes have higher fitness. In effect, the fitness function is the 'environment' to which the population adapts. A candidate solution's 'genotype' is its chromosome, and its 'phenotype' is its fitness. By analogy with natural selection, lower fitness candidates are then replaced in the population with new solutions modeled on higher fitness candidates. New candidates are generated by modifying earlier candidates with 'mutations' that randomly change chromosomal elements and 'crossover' events that combine pieces of two chromosomes. After reproducing variants of the fittest candidates for many generations, the population contains better and better solutions.

Swarm Intelligence

Many organisms live in *social groups*, and artificial life uses bottom-up models to explore how the structure and behavior of social groups arises and is controlled. The simplest examples concern the social organization of insects. Distributed networks of relatively simple insects give rise to complex collective behaviors, involving foraging, nest building, transporting resources, and the like. These collective behaviors are remarkably flexible, robust and autonomous. The attempt to design algorithms or distributed problem-solving methods inspired by the collective behavior of insect societies has come to be called *swarm intelligence*.

Individual ants are not smart, but ant colonies are. A colony can solve problems unthinkable for individual ants, such as finding the shortest path to the best food source, allocating workers to different tasks, or defending a territory from neighbors. As individuals, ants might be tiny dummies, but as colonies they respond quickly and effectively to their environment. Their swarm intelligence relies upon countless interactions between individual ants, each of which is following simple rules of thumb. Scientists describe such a system as *self-organizing*. When looking for a role model in a world of complexity, imitating a colony of ants or bees is not the worst option.

Recent advances in swarm intelligence include a theory of how groups of robots work together to solve group goals involving robot swarms. In robotics *swarm-bots* are a collection of mobile robots able to self-assemble and to self-organize in order to solve problems that cannot be solved by a single robot. These robots combine the power of swarm intelligence with the flexibility of self-reconfiguration because aggregate swarm-bots can dynamically change their structure to match environmental variations. SWARM-BOTS, a project funded by the Future and Emerging Technologies program of the European Union, focuses on the design and the implementation of self-organizing and self-assembling biologically-inspired robots.

Drawing heavily on the chemical biology, researchers from Humboldt University in Germany have devised a way for electronic agents to efficiently *assemble a network without* having to rely on *a central plan*. The researchers modeled their idea on the methods of insects and other life-forms whose communications lack central planning, but who manage to form networks when individuals secrete and respond to chemical trails. The researchers found that what works for ants and bacteria also works for autonomous pieces of computer code. Rather than determining the structure of a network in a top-down approach of hierarchical planning, agents found nodes and created connections in a bottom-up process of self-organization.

5.7.1 Craig Venter Creates Synthetic Life Form

In May 2010, Craig Venter and his crack team of scientists successfully created a synthetic life form for the first time ever using a custom-made string of DNA. This is one of the milestones in the history of science. Venter and his team used the bioinformatics tool to design the chromosome, synthesized it using the four building blocks of life written into its DNA (the bases Adenine, Guanine, Cytosine and Thymine) and then assembled it in yeast before transplanting it into a recipient bacterial cell. This bacterial cell was then transformed into a new bacterial species. The new species they created has some extraordinary elements in its genome including a website!! It is a living species now, part of our planet's inventory of life. It is the first synthetic cell with a computer as its parent. This is certainly a defining moment in the history of biology and biotechnology. Craig Venter was not merely copying life artificially or modifying it radically by genetic engineering. He played the role of a god: creating artificial life that could never have existed naturally. The new organism is based on an existing bacterium that causes mastitis in goats, but at its core is an entirely synthetic genome that was constructed from chemicals in the laboratory.

The research has occupied 20 scientists for more than 10 years at an estimated cost of $40 m.The achievement may herald the dawn of a new era, in which new life is made to benefit humanity. Early applications might be bacteria that churn out biofuels, soak up carbon dioxide from the atmosphere and even manufacture vaccines.

The team now plans to use the synthetic organism to work out the minimum number of genes needed for life to exist. From this, new microorganisms could be made by bolting on additional genes to produce useful chemicals, break down pollutants, or produce proteins for use in vaccines.

According to Venter, "Over the next 20 years, synthetic genomics may become the standard for making anything". "The chemical industry will depend on it. Hopefully, a large part of the energy industry will depend on it. We really need to find an alternative to taking carbon out of the ground, burning it, and putting it into the atmosphere. That is the single biggest contribution I could make."

Practical Applications of Artificial Life

One measure for the success of a scientific field is its usefulness for solving practical problems. By this criterion, artificial life is a success today, mainly because of applications that exploit genetic algorithms and offshoots like genetic programming. Biologically-inspired methods are increasingly applied to technological problems, such as using immune-system principles and mechanisms to protect computer systems against attacks by computer viruses and worms, and designing novel strategies for navigation of autonomous flight systems. The increased understanding of real biological systems has allowed us to control them better. For example, artificial life is helping to illuminate why normal cells evolve into cancerous cells. Finally, artificial life is used for a variety of aesthetic purposes. There are artificial-life approaches to music composition, and the techno-artists' journal Leonardo regularly publishes papers concerning ALife.

Conclusions

Artificial life is an interdisciplinary investigation into one of the most fundamental aspect of the natural world—life itself. Its synthetic methodology is making incremental progress on a wide range of issues, from dynamical hierarchies and artificial cells to the evolution of complexity. Its ambitious agenda for the future involves explaining how life arises from non-living substrates, determining the potentials and limits of living systems. This agenda means that artificial life is likely to change the future face of cognitive science in significant ways.

5.8 Artificial Consciousness and Emotions

Since the appearance of computer technology, computer scientists have dreamed about building a conscious robot. The big issue is whether this is feasible even in principle. Is consciousness a prerogative of human beings, which depends on the material the brain is made of or can be replicated using different hardware? Given the results of artificial intelligence and neural computing, in the near future machines may exceed human intelligence and develop a mind. If human consciousness is attributable to complex neural electro-chemical interactions in the brain, it could become just a matter of time until a machine can achieve self-awareness.

A crucial question is whether consciousness can be linked to the biological portion of our intelligence. Will future machines be capable of having emotional and spiritual experience? It may be expected that nonbiological entities will claim to have emotional and spiritual experiences. However, there does not yet exist an objective test that can conclusively determine the presence of consciousness. The core of consciousness, subjective experience, cannot thus far be penetrated through objective measurement. Only behavioral correlates of consciousness have been identified. The presence of behavior resulting from consciousness does not necessarily imply a thing being alive. Conversely, the absence of behavioral indications of consciousness does not necessarily point to something not being alive.

Because issues of consciousness cannot be resolved at the moment through objective measurement a critical role exists for philosophy. The nature of subjective experience is also fundamental to our concepts of ethics, morality and law.

There is no consensus among humans about the consciousness of non-human entities. But our future nonbiological replicas will be vastly more intelligent and therefore will exhibit the finer qualities of human thought to a far greater degree. These nonbiological entities will be extremely intelligent so that they can likely convince other humans that they are conscious using all of the emotional cues that humans employ.

5.8.1 Forms of Consciousness

A number of distinct forms of consciousness are observable in humans.

Anesthesia: When a patient is subjected to general anesthesia e.g., for open heart surgery, all behavioral indications of consciousness stop during the procedure. Sometimes patients can remember things that occurred during the surgery, suggesting there may be some level of consciousness. But we cannot ascertain whether the patient is conscious or not.

Sleep: During deep sleep, breathing becomes regular, brain activity is reduced and the person (generally) stops interacting with the environment. But persons can respond in this state. They can be awakened by being shaken, from hearing a loud noise, someone speaking their name, the lights being turned on, a sharp pain, etc.... Persons often recall having dreams, and can be awakened by events that occur in a dream. The person is alive, but we cannot always make behavioral measurements that would suggest an alive state.

REM sleep is the fifth of the five stages of sleep most people go through each night. REM is characterized by *rapid eyes movements* during sleep, which is what gave this stage its name. During REM sleep, the large voluntary muscles of the body are paralyzed, but brain activity is quite intense. REM sleep is the stage of sleep when people have intense dreams. During REM sleep, breathing and heart rate are faster than normal. The sleeper's legs, face, and fingers are trembling and there is rapid movement of the eyes. The stages of sleep proceed in cycles throughout the night. The cycles may repeat as many as five times per night. The length and intensity of REM sleep increase with each succeeding cycle. During the first cycle, REM sleep might be only 10 min long, while during the last cycle it might stretch to 90 min.

Cryonics is the freezing of the human body and brain. A person walks into Cryonics Inc. and asks to be frozen, perhaps because he can no longer be sustained by contemporary medicine and has the hope that healing and reanimation may be possible in the future. Cryonics Inc. administers a lethal cocktail, and then proceeds to quickly drain her fluids and pack her in ice. Many years later, they repair crystal damage, and revive her. From the person's perspective, she got a lethal injection and died. The freezing of the body/brain is irrelevant.

When the person is revived, that individual is alive and it may be considered to be the same individual. From the revived person's point of view, she will have been handed all the previous person's memories, body, and substrates to generate an identical copy of her previous consciousness. She must be considered as a replica, because the original died many years ago. In fact, the new version will remember the lethal injection. It will not sense the passage of time, because there was nothing alive all those previous years. There is no observable behavior, indicating an alive state in the original person, once frozen. The new version represented electronically is, hopefully, a good approximation of the original, and may behave almost identically. The future repair technologies expected by cryonics are still hypothetical. As of 2010, only around 200 people have undergone the procedure. In the USA, cryonics can only be legally preformed on humans after they have been declared legally dead, as otherwise it would count as murder or assisted suicide.

Split Brain. In some severe cases of epilepsy, doctors sometimes performed surgery to cut the corpus collosum (connective neurons between left and right hemispheres). Split brain patients appear to function and behave normally after this dramatic surgery. However, anecdotal reports and careful testing reveal that there are two conscious entities inside the body after this procedure. Each hemisphere controls the opposite half of the body, and only senses that half. Presenting things to one hemisphere, through its half of the visual field, is only perceived by that hemisphere. In this case, there are two people, taken from parts of the original person prior to the surgery. No death has occurred. Rather, the personal identity of the original person has changed from one singular person to two similar persons.

Hypnosis. Hypnosis is considered mostly a distinctly altered state of consciousness. Electroencephalographic (EEG) studies indicate that during hypnosis subjects are not in a sleeplike state but are awake, though sometimes a bit drowsy. They can freely resist the hypnotist's suggestions and are far from mindless automatons. If hypnosis differs in kind rather than in degree from ordinary consciousness, it could imply that hypnotized people can take actions that would be impossible to perform in the waking state. It could also lend credibility to claims that hypnosis is a unique means of reducing pain or of effecting psychological and medical cures.

5.8.2 Problem of Consciousness

Consciousness is a term that refers to the relationship between the mind and the world with which it interacts. It has been defined as: subjectivity, awareness, the ability to experience or to feel, wakefulness, having a sense of selfhood, and the executive control system of the mind. We have seen that there are several states of consciousness that a human experiences. Despite the difficulty in definition, many philosophers believe that there is a broadly shared underlying intuition about what consciousness is. Anything that we are aware of at a given moment forms part of our consciousness, making conscious experience a familiar but mysterious aspect of our lives.

The problem of consciousness is the central issue in current theorizing about the mind. The mind requires a complex dynamic system in the background, like a brain, to operate within the reach of a physical environment. Mind is the stream of consciousness. Despite the lack of any agreed upon theory of consciousness, there is a widespread consensus that an adequate account of mind requires a clear understanding of consciousness and its place in nature and reality.

Questions about the nature of conscious awareness have been asked for as long as there have been humans. By the beginning of the seventeenth century, consciousness had become central in thinking about the mind. Philosophers like John Locke (1688) regarded consciousness as essential to thought as well as to personal identity. For most of the next two centuries the domains of thought and consciousness were regarded as more or less the same.

In the 1980s and 1990s there was a major resurgence of scientific and philosophical research into the nature and basis of consciousness. The words "conscious" and "consciousness" are umbrella terms that cover a wide variety of mental phenomena. An animal, person or other cognitive system may be regarded as conscious in a number of different ways.

Sentience: Consciousness may lie in the ability to feel, perceive or have subjective experiences. Being conscious in this sense may admit of different degrees, and just what sort of sensory capacities are sufficient may not be sharply defined. Are fish conscious in this respect? What about shrimp or bees?

Wakefulness: One might count an organism as conscious only if it were awake and normally alert. Hence, organisms would not count as conscious when asleep or in any of the deeper levels of coma. Again boundaries may be blurry, and intermediate cases may exist.

Self-consciousness: A more demanding standard might define conscious creatures as those that are not only aware, but also aware that they are aware, so that consciousness is a form of *self-consciousness*. The self-awareness requirement might be interpreted in a variety of ways, and which creatures would qualify as conscious in the relevant sense will vary accordingly.

What it is like: According to Nagel (1974), a being is conscious just if there is "something that it is like" to be that creature, i.e. some subjective way the world seems or appears from the creature's mental or experiential point of view. He states that "an organism has conscious mental states if and only if there is something that it is like to *be* that organism—something it is like *for* the organism."

Transitive Consciousness: Creatures may be described as conscious as being *conscious of* various things involving some object at which consciousness is directed.

There are thus many concepts of consciousness, and both "conscious" and "consciousness" are used in a wide range of ways with no privileged meaning. Consciousness is a complex feature of the world, and understanding it will require a diversity of conceptual tools for dealing with its many differing aspects.

Understanding consciousness involves a multiplicity not only of explanations but also of questions that they pose and the sorts of answers they require. The relevant questions can be gathered under three crude rubrics as the What, How, and Why questions.

The Descriptive Question: *What* is consciousness? What are its principal features? And by what means can they best be discovered, described and modeled?

The Explanatory Question: *How* does consciousness of the relevant sort come to exist? Is it a primitive aspect of reality, and if not how does (or could) consciousness arise from or be caused by non-conscious entities or processes?

The Functional Question: *Why* does consciousness exist? Does it have a function, and if so what it is it? Does it act causally and if so with what sorts of effects? Does it make a difference to the operation of systems in which it is present, and if so why and how?

Chalmers (1995) makes a distinction between the hard and easy problems of consciousness. The hard problem is the problem of explaining the relationship between physical phenomena, such as brain processes, and experience. It is the problem of explaining how and why people have qualitative phenomenal experiences. Why are physical processes ever accompanied by experience? Why is there a subjective component to experience? Why does awareness of sensory information exist? These are formulations of the hard problem. Providing an answer to these questions could lie in understanding the roles that physical processes play in creating consciousness, and the extent to which these processes create subjective qualities of experience.

The hard problem contrasts with so-called *easy problems*. The easy problems of consciousness try to explain the ability to discriminate, categorize, and react to environmental stimuli; the integration of information by a cognitive system, the report ability of mental states, the ability of a system to access its own internal states, the focus of attention, the deliberate control of behavior, and the difference between wakefulness and sleep.

All of these phenomena are vulnerable to functional explanation in terms of computational or neural mechanisms, although there is not yet anything close to a complete explanation of any of these phenomena. But the really hard problem of consciousness is the problem of experience. For example, when we see there is the experience of visual sensations: the felt quality of redness, the experience of dark and light, the quality of depth in a visual field. Other experiences go along with, for example the sound of a clarinet, or the smell of mothballs. Then there are bodily sensations, from pains to orgasms, mental images that are conjured up internally, the felt quality of emotion, and the experience of a stream of conscious thought. All of these states are united in that there is something it is like to be in them. All of them are states of experience.

What makes the hard problem hard and almost unique is that it goes *beyond* the performance of functions. Once the performance of all the cognitive and behavioral functions relating to experience has been explained, there may still remain the further unanswered question: *Why is the performance of these functions accompanied by experience?*

A widely-held opinion is that experiences cannot be fully explained in purely physical terms. This is sometimes expressed as the claim that there is an *explanatory gap* (Levine 1983) between the physical and the phenomenal world of experiences.

There is no consensus about the status of the explanatory gap. Some deny that the gap exists and hold that consciousness is an entirely physical phenomenon. They argue that once the easy problems are solved, there will be nothing left to be explained about consciousness (Dennett 2005). In contrast, Chalmers argues that the problem of experience will persist even when the performance of all the relevant functions is explained, and a new approach is needed to cross the explanatory gap.

Perhaps the most popular extra ingredient that has been proposed is quantum mechanics. Many physicists contend that quantum mechanics could be enough for building up a consistent theory of consciousness (Georgiev 2004). The attractiveness of quantum theories of consciousness may stem from a Law of Minimization of Mystery: consciousness is mysterious and quantum mechanics is mysterious, so maybe the two mysteries have a common source.

However, according to Chalmers, quantum theories of consciousness suffer from the same difficulties as neural or computational theories. Quantum phenomena have some remarkable functional properties, such as non-determinism and non-locality. These properties may play some role in the explanation of cognitive functions, such as random choice and the integration of information, and this hypothesis cannot be ruled out a priori. But when it comes to the explanation of experience, quantum processes are in the same boat as any other. The question of why these processes should give rise to experience is entirely unanswered and they offer no hope of *explaining* consciousness in terms of quantum processes. Rather, these theories *assume* the existence of consciousness, and use it in the explanation of quantum processes. At best, these theories tell something about a physical role that consciousness may play. They say nothing about how it arises. At the end of the day, the same criticism applies to *any* purely physical account of consciousness.

Chalmers suggests that a theory of consciousness should take experience as a fundamental property of the universe, like mass, electromagnetic change, and spacetime. A new psycho-physical theory would relate psycho-physical processes and experience. These psychophysical principles, connecting the properties of physical processes to the properties of experience, can not interfere with physical laws, but rather would be a supplement to a physical theory.

5.8.3 The Irrelevance of Quantum Computing for Consciousness

Many researchers have conjectured that quantum effects in the brain are crucial for explaining psychological phenomena, including consciousness. However, recent research has indicated that computation via quantum mechanical processes is not necessary to explain consciousness. Due to the enormous computing power of neurons, consciousness can still be explained within a purely neurobiological framework, without requiring the assumption of quantum computation. Thus, it may be argued that neuro-computational rather than quantum mechanisms provide the most credible explanations of mental phenomena. In short, while quantum effects exist in any physical process, an appeal to quantum effects does not seem to contribute to understanding how consciousness arises.

An analogy would be the use of quantum effects to understand how it is that birds can fly. It is unnecessary to refer to atomic bonding properties of birds to explain the wing function in their flight (Litt et al. 2006). Although most wing feathers are made of keratin, which has specific bonding properties, the wing function can be explained independently of this atomic structure. For bird–flight, aerodynamic mechanisms, such as geometry, stiffness, and strength are much more relevant to explain the flight of birds, even though atomic bonding properties may give rise to specific geometric and tensile properties. Clarifying how birds fly does not require specification of how atoms bond in feathers. Explaining brain function by appeal to quantum mechanics is akin to explaining bird flight by appeal to atomic bonding characteristics.

Furthermore, there are three principal arguments for the implausibility of quantum mechanical processes in brain operation. The first argument is computational. Quantum effects do not have the temporal properties required for neural information processing. Certainly, phenomena which require quantum mechanical explanation do exist throughout the brain, and are fundamental to any complete understanding of its structure and physical mechanics. Every molecular bond and chemical interaction has non-negligible quantum effects. However, quantum effects do not contribute essentially to explaining the overall functionality of the brain. Information processing in the brain can be appropriately described without reference to quantum theory. Specifically, quantum-level events, in particular the super positional coherences necessary for quantum computation, do not have the temporal endurance to control neural-based information processing. The fastest firing neurons work on millisecond timescales, while polarization excitations in even the shortest microtubules in quantum computation are on the order of 10^{-7} s. Therefore, a functional explanation of the brain need not resort to quantum mechanisms. For the general operations of the brain, quantum effects are at a sufficiently low level so that any associated fluctuations can be categorized and handled as noise.

The second argument against quantum consciousness is biological: there are substantial physical obstacles to any organic instantiation of quantum computation. Although significant progress has been made in the design and production of large-scale quantum computers, the required working conditions contrast vividly with the immediate environment of the brain (Vandersypen et al. 2001).

The advantage of a quantum computer is its ability to maintain superposed qubit (a qubit, or quantum bit, is the unit of quantum information allowing two values of 0 and 1 at the same time) states long enough to facilitate super parallel computation. However, a vital prerequisite for preventing decoherence (loss of coherence between the components of a system) is the maintenance of a very high degree of isolation from even minute environmental interactions. Exceedingly low operational temperatures are also a necessity for most physical implementations of quantum computers, although simpler machines based on nuclear magnetic resonance have managed room-temperature coherence over useful timescales (Cory et al. 1997). The conditions that exist in and around brains do not conform to these physical requirements and would likely instantaneously cause disruption and end quantum coherence.

Another important physical obstacle to quantum computation in the brain is the matter of *error correction*, which pertains to noise tolerance in the transmission and processing of information. Although redundant networks (with some extra capacity if certain components fail) may also play a role, the most common brain implementations of error correction and recovery seem to involve either tuned attractor boundaries or high-precision spike codes (relationship between stimuli in the form of electrical pulses and neuronal responses) which are well-understood engineering concepts (Stiber and Holderman 2004).

Although nature is capable of evolving ingenious solutions to difficult problems, the burden of proof is on those who would invoke quantum mechanics to not only provide the details of such a biological mechanism for quantum error correction, but to do so in the face of physical evidence for simpler, classically based alternatives. Even if quantum computation in the brain were technically feasible, there is still a question about the need for such massive computational efficiency in explaining the mind. No evidence has been generated that brains need the power of quantum parallelism to support the basic biological needs of survival and reproduction.

The third argument against a quantum basis for consciousness is psychological. It has been proposed that there may be psychological phenomena such as conscious experience, which are not amenable to a neurocomputational explanation but that may be explicable by appeal to quantum theory (Penrose 1994, 1997; Hamerhoff 1998a, b). The effect of anesthesia has been invoked as evidence for a quantum mechanical theory of consciousness (Hamerhoff 1998a). However, in recent years, explanations of anesthetics based on molecular biology have received substantial empirical support. None of these explanatory mechanisms involve quantum computation (Litt et al. 2006). Hence, anesthesia does not provide empirical support for quantum computation with regard to consciousness.

All of the evidence points to the conclusion that understanding consciousness is unlikely to require quantum computation. The scientific exploration of consciousness is still in its infancy, but there is no evidence to suggest any superiority of quantum mechanical over neurocomputational explanations. Therefore, the onus is on the proponents of quantum theory to show that aspects of the brain cannot be explained by neurocomputational theories, and that they need explanation by quantum computation.

5.8.4 Relationship Between Intelligence and Consciousness

Humans are both conscious and intelligent. However, it is possible to imagine one attribute without the other. An intelligent but unconscious being is known as a "zombie" in both science fiction and philosophy. It is also possible to imagine a conscious non-intelligent being. It would experience its environment as a flow of unidentified, meaningless sensations engendering no mental activity beyond mere passive awareness. Digital computers will almost certainly be intelligent at some time in the future. We may then live in a world full of zombies, with all of the resulting moral and philosophical issues.

The majority opinion in biology and neuroscience is that consciousness results from the chemical and physical structure of humans, just as photosynthesis results from the chemistry of plants. A computer is made of the wrong material for consciousness to arise. In this view, digital computers will never be conscious, even if they are intelligent.

However, some researchers do believe that, once computers and software grow powerful and sophisticated enough, they will be conscious as well as intelligent. They point to a similarity between neurons, the brain's basic component, and transistors, the basic component of computers. Both neurons and transistors transform incoming electrical signals to outgoing signals. While a single neuron is not conscious and not intelligent, the brain of a conscious and intelligent human is. A single transistor is similarly not conscious. But gather many together, connect them and you will get consciousness, just as with neurons. Furthermore, if a type of consciousness exists that is different from our own, we may fail to recognize it because human consciousness is the only kind we know.

The possibility of machine consciousness raises a number of important issues.

Why build a self-aware machine?

A strong motivation would certainly come from the innate human desire to discover new horizons and to extend the frontiers of science. Also, developing an artificial brain based on the same principles as used in the biological brain would provide a way for transferring the human mind into a faster and more robust door to immortality.

If the hypothesis of consciousness as a physical property of the brain is supported and human consciousness is an electrical neural state spontaneously developed by complex brains, then the possibility of realizing artificial self-aware beings remains open.

Will machines ever become human?

One day, computer programs may become so complex and processing speeds become so great that for all intents and purposes it will appear that computers are actually 'thinking'. Could this process of 'thinking' develop to the point where a computer becomes self-aware? A discussion of this issue requires distinguishing between three distinct concepts: 'thinking', 'intelligence', and 'self-awareness'. Each of these represents a different threshold for machines to attain.

Thinking refers to making decisions, selecting from a set of options, examining consequences, determining what is true and what is false, deciding on a course of action, problem solving, etc. Computers, no matter how complex, do not plan ahead and make decisions. They may be programmed to select the best option from an array of possibilities, but are unable to consider any options other than those that are programmed in. A computer must run through every possibility before coming up with an answer, and it is unable to ignore certain moves as being poor until it actually works through them. In contrast, a human can think; he is able to make leaps of judgment without the need to slavishly run through all the calculations.

A distinction must be made between knowledge and *intelligence*. Knowledge is the knowing of things, having a collection of data. Although computers possess a great deal of knowledge in their data banks, computers do not 'know' they have knowledge, as a person does. This is where intelligence comes in, that is the knowing of things, not just having the knowledge of things. Some computers do contain a great deal of knowledge, but do not 'know' anything and they cannot be described as being intelligent.

Humans are *self-aware* because we know that we exist and are aware of our surroundings and what is happening around us. Computers obviously cannot know that they exist, so they cannot possess self-awareness. Some would argue that when computers reach a certain level of complexity they will become self-aware. If it is simply a matter of complexity, then the day will surely come when computers will be self-aware. However, there is more to achieving self-awareness than just increasing the degree of complexity of computation that is feasible. The main difference is how we solve problems. While the human has understanding, the computer just has programs and rules.

One approach for identifying the ingredients for self-awareness is to examine biological life. This would include viruses, which possess the ability to self-replicate. DNA and RNA are macromolecules and constitute the foundation of all life on this planet, and thus would seem to form a precondition for all minds on this planet. But DNA and RNA do not have minds, they are not even alive, and are essentially just robots, with no intentionality behind their actions.

Nevertheless, these mindless little molecular robots form the basis for human consciousness; humans are the direct descendants of these self-replicating robots. We are mammals and have descended from reptiles, which descended from fish, whose ancestors were marine worm-like creatures, who descended from simpler multi-celled creatures who descended from single celled creatures who descended from self-replicating macromolecules, about three billion years ago. To put it more starkly, our great, great, great….grandmother was a robot! We are not only descended from macromolecules but are composed of them. Each of our cells—a tiny agent that can perform only a limited number of tasks—is about as mindless as a virus. Enough of these dumb little machines have been combined to result in a real, conscious person, with a genuine mind. We *are* made of a collection of trillions of macromolecular machines, which in turn are ultimately descended from the original self-replicating macromolecules. So something made of dumb, mindless robots *can* exhibit genuine consciousness, we are living proof of that.

The only difference between mindless machines, or macromolecules, and a 'mind', is *intentionality*—the ability to act by conscious decision. To gain an understanding of how we make conscious decisions it may be useful to look at the way in which computers work. A thermostat performs the same function as a computer, it will take in data, check if certain conditions are met, and then proceed to the next stage. The device registers whether the temperature is greater or smaller than the setting, and then arranges for the circuit to be disconnected in the former case and connected in the latter. It is carrying out an algorithm, a calculational procedure. A computer is a machine that is designed to carry out algorithms, it computes! Any procedure that can be converted into an algorithm, can be executed by a computer. In the case of the thermostat the algorithm is very simple, computers execute far more complex algorithms, and the human brain performs even vastly more complex algorithms.

According to some of the enthusiasts of artificial intelligence, the human brain only differs from a thermostat in that it is much more complicated. All mental qualities, such as intelligence, thinking, understanding, consciousness, are merely features of the algorithm carried out by the brain. If an algorithm exists that matches what takes place in a human brain, then it could in principle be run on a computer with sufficient storage space and speed of operation. If such an algorithm was installed into a computer it would, presumably, pass the Turing test and respond in every way comparable to how a human being would respond. Whenever the algorithm were run it would, some supporters of artificial intelligence argue, experience feelings, have consciousness and be a mind.

However, some skeptics about artificial intelligence argue that mere complexity of operation is not in itself enough to generate consciousness and does not allow for the computation of complex algorithms with any understanding. They argue, quite rightly, that a thermostat has no understanding or knowledge of what it does, nor does a car, an airplane or a space shuttle, the latter being many, many times more complex than a thermostat!

With the advances being made in computer technology, computers will reach the same level of complexity as the human brain by around the year 2029. Once that level of complexity has been reached, the issue is to determine if the computer really is self-aware. It will not be possible to establish self-awareness on the basis of the Turing test approach, because it will not be known if the answers the computer gives are due to it being intelligent, or simply due to good programming. One way to establish computer awareness, which would not provide definitive proof, but at least it would be a very strong indicator, might be the following. By simply switching the computer on and not running any specific program, would it come up with any new ideas of its own accord? If after an unspecified period of doing nothing, the computer announced that it had been studying quantum theory and made a suggestion for a new line of experimental enquiry that should produce such and such results, then that would be a strong candidate for self-awareness. However, this would not be completely convincing, because such a line of enquiry could have been pre-programmed. Perhaps it would be more interesting if the computer started writing its own programs and that might be considered to be the equivalent of exercising free will.

If a computer does at some point become self-aware, how would it manage to convince us that it is? One possibility is that it could go on strike until we grant it recognition, but then that could just be part of the program designed to it. This also raises the interesting question, are *all of us* just running a program?

There is no test that we can apply to a computer to determine beyond all doubt that it is self-aware. In using the Turing test a computer may respond in a manner that a person is expected to respond, and the computer *acts* as if it were self-aware.

Conclusions

If human consciousness is the result of complex neural-chemical interactions, the possibility that machines will develop a mind is becoming more realistic. Given the current pace of computer evolution and the progress in artificial neural networks, scientists predict that computing systems will reach the complexity of the human brain around 2029. On the one hand, it is still unclear whether there is any true possibility of reproducing consciousness in a machine. On the other hand there is no known law of nature that forbids the existence of subjective feelings in artefacts designed by humans.

The implication of developing an artificial brain is that it would provide a way for transferring our mind into a faster and more robust support mechanism, opening a door toward immortality. Freed from a fragile and degradable body, human beings with synthetic organs could represent the next evolutionary step of the human race. Such a new species could start the exploration of the universe, search for alien civilizations, survive to the death of the solar system and perhaps escape from it, control the energy of black holes and move at the speed of light in search for the human survival on other planets. All of this depends on the ability keep technology under control and making sure that it is used to the benefit of human civilization.

5.8.5 Artificial Emotions

Since it is believed that emotions play a significant role in problem solving and decision making (Damasio 1995), research in Artificial Intelligence and Artificial Life is directing some attention on emotions. The concept of artificial emotion is increasingly used in designing autonomous robotic agents, mostly by making robots respond emotionally to situations experienced in the world or to interactions with humans. According to Michaud et al. (2000) emotions can serve three important roles in designing autonomous robots.

Emotions to Adapt to Limitations: Emotions play a role in determining control in different forms of behavior, in particular in coordinating plans and multiple goals to adapt to the contingencies of the world. In the adaptation process of humans in the world, emotions help to find an equilibrium between the subject's concerns and the environment. Uncertainty prevents a complete dependence on predictive models in human planning, and argues in favor of the design of artificial emotions.

Emotions for Managing Social Behavior: In social behavior, emotions are associated with four universal problems of adaptation: hierarchy (Anger/Fear), territoriality (Exploration/Surprise), identity (Acceptance/Rejection) and temporality (Joy/Sadness). Emotions may be viewed as functional adaptations in establishing a balance of opposing forces in social transactions. These balances are always temporary and frequently change when moving from one conflict to another.

Emotions for Interpersonal Communication: In order to regulate behavior in social interaction, emotions also have a communicative role. They act to release the coordination of social behavior in order to promote group cohesion, to communicate about the external environment, and about threat signals. It is advantageous to communicate intentions to others, and to be sensitive to messages from others. Emotional expression may promote individual or group isolation (as it may be necessary in defending something) or promote group formation (as different social circumstances might require). Emotion then serves a dual purpose: it is a both an act of communication and a sensory state.

From an engineering point of view, autonomous robots would surely benefit from having emotional mechanisms that play a similar role in humans. The long term research goal is to propose a model of artificial emotion that is suitable for robots to behave autonomously in their environment. In addition, different mechanisms for implementing artificial emotions can surely be designed according to properties associated with the decision making approach used to control a robot.

AI research in emotions with HCI tries to optimize the relationship between the human user and machines, by developing engineering tools to measure, model, and provide responses to human emotions through sensors, algorithms, and hardware devices. Moreover, research into *Intelligent Agents* bases its internal architectures on emotions (*emotion-based systems*) as biologically inspired processes. Its main objective is to emulate emotion processes in agents' behavior.

Both of these branches of research aim to improve system performance in decision making, action selection, behavior control, trustworthiness, and autonomy. However, since these branches of research are new and very complex, it is not surprising that their projects are confronted with basic problems.

5.9 Artificial Stupidity

Artificial Stupidity is the term commonly used as a humorous contrast to Artificial Intelligence. The term is often used to refer derogatorily to the inability of an AI program to adequately perform basic tasks. But artificial stupidity also refers to decreasing the intellectual content of computer programs by deliberately introducing errors in their responses when they attempt to pass the Turing test. In 1991, when the first Loebner prize competition was run, *The Economist* reported that the winning entry incorporated deliberate errors to fool the judges into believing that it was human. This technique has remained a part of the subsequent Loebner prize competitions. A sufficiently developed Artificial Stupidity program would enable computer programmers to find flaws in programs in the development and debugging stages of computer software.

6 Artificial Intelligence in Economics

Artificial, or Computational, Economics is a research discipline at the interface between computer science and economics. Within the area of computational economics the field of Agent-based Computational Economics (ACE) belongs to the discipline of complex adaptive dynamic systems that studies economic processes, including whole economies, as dynamic systems of autonomous interacting agents. Large numbers of individual agents engage repeatedly in local interactions, giving rise to global regularities such as employment and growth rates, income distributions, market institutions, and social conventions. These global regularities in turn feed back into the determination of local interactions. The result is an intricate system of interdependent feedback loops connecting microeconomic behaviors, interaction patterns, and global regularities. Recent advances in analytical and computational tools, taking into account these kinds of aspects, allowed the emergence of the ACE approach.

Agent-based modeling offers some advantages relative to other methodologies for economic research. More complex phenomena and larger economies can be considered than with behavioral laboratory experiments. Some underlying structural parameters of an economy, such as demand, production, and cost functions, and therefore equilibrium prices and quantities, can be directly observed, rather than estimated, as would be required if real-world data were used. Point predictions of theoretical models can be computed. Moreover, in addition to observing the underlying structure of the economy, the researcher can specify and control it. The researcher can evaluate a change in one parameter while keeping all else constant and look at its effect in isolation. In the real world, in contrast, such changes often occur concurrently with changes in other variables. The ability to vary one parameter exogenously allows the direction of causality to be established in the relationship between two variables.

ACE is well-suited to studying *complex* systems. A system is defined to be complex if it is composed of interacting units and the system exhibits *emergent* properties, that is, properties arising from the interactions of the units that are not properties of the individual units themselves.

The complexity that is embraced by ACE research makes it difficult, if not impossible, to use conventional methods for introduction of new theories, such as stating and proving theorems. Instead, much ACE research uses computer simulations to analyze complex dynamic models. There has been, and will almost surely continue to be, tremendous progress in improving computer hardware. There has also been significant progress in software engineering, which is particularly valuable for ACE modeling.

A *complex adaptive* system typically includes the following features:

- It includes *reactive* units which are capable of demonstrating systematically different attributes due to changed environmental conditions.
- It includes *goal-directed* units which direct some of their reactions towards the achievement of built-in (or evolved) goals.
- It includes *planner* units that attempt to exert some degree of control over their environment to facilitate achievement of these goals.

The agents in an ACE model can be economic entities as well as social, biological, and physical entities. In ACE, the term agent refers broadly to an encapsulated piece of software that includes data together with behavioral methods that act on these data. Some of these data are publicly accessible to all other agents. Others are designated as private, and hence are not accessible by any other agents, or only accessible to a specified subset of other agents. Agents can communicate with each other through public and/or private channels, depending on the economy that is considered.

Examples of agents include individuals (e.g., consumers, workers), social groupings (e.g., families, firms, government agencies), institutions (e.g., markets, regulatory systems), biological entities (e.g., crops, livestock, forests), and physical entities (e.g., infrastructure, weather, and geographical regions). Thus, agents can range from active data gathering decision-makers with sophisticated learning capabilities, to passive structures with no cognitive functioning. Moreover, hierarchical constructions are permitted, so that, e.g., a firm might be composed of workers and managers.

ACE consists of two branches. One branch is descriptive, focusing on the explanation of emergent global behavior. Why have particular global regularities evolved and persisted in real-world decentralized market economies, despite the absence of top-down planning and control? How and why have these global regularities been generated, through the repeated local interactions of autonomous interacting agents? The second branch is normative, with a focus on the discovery of alternative economic designs that might increase consumer surplus, seller profit, or overall welfare. For a particular economic entity, what are the implications of that entity for the performance of the economy as a whole? For example, how might a particular market protocol or government regulation affect economic efficiency?

The ACE focus on self-organizing systems is not new. Traditional economics has studied the specific processes whereby social order can emerge from self-interested micro-level behavior, with theoretical, empirical, and experimental methods. What is new about ACE is its use of powerful new computational tools in four key ways (Tesfatsion 2001, 2002, 2003).

1. Computational systems are constructed. They are populated with heterogeneous agents, who determine their interactions with other agents and with their environment on the basis of social norms, behavioral rules, and data acquired through experience.
2. Agents continually adapt their behavior in order to satisfy their preferences. In this way the economic world exhibits self-organization.
3. The evolutionary process is considered as a process of natural selection which directly acts on agent behavior, and invites agents to open-ended experimentation with new behavioral rules. This allows agents co-evolve in the economy.
4. The economic worlds modeled can grow in real time, and new events, driven by agent–agent and agent-environment interactions without further outside intervention, can be included.

In ACE, the traditional mathematical optimization by agents is replaced by the less restrictive and more behaviorally plausible postulate of boundedly rational agents adapting to market forces. ACE models apply numerical methods of analysis to computer-based simulations of complex dynamic problems for which more conventional methods may not be adequate.

Starting from initial conditions, which include type characteristics, internalized behavioral norms and modes of behavior (including modes of communication and learning), and internally stored information about itself and other agents, the computational economy evolves over time as its constituent agents repeatedly interact with each other, without further intervention from the modeler. Agents learn and modify behavior in response to the activity they observe. These local interactions give rise to macroeconomic regularities such as shared market protocols and behavioral norms which in turn feed back into the determination of local interactions. All events that subsequently occur must arise from the historical time-line of agent-agent interactions. The result is a complicated dynamic system of recurrent causal chains, connecting individual behaviors, interaction networks, and social welfare outcomes. Therefore, ACE has been characterized as a bottom-up approach to the study of economic systems.

This intricate two-way feedback between microstructure and macrostructure has been recognized within economics for a very long time, but economists have mostly lacked the means to model this feedback quantitatively in its full dynamic complexity. Traditional quantitative economic models have relied heavily on extraneous coordination devices such as fixed decision rules, common knowledge assumptions, representative agents, and imposed market equilibrium constraints.

However, researchers now have a new approach to quantitatively model a wide variety of complex phenomena associated with decentralized market economies, such as inductive learning, imperfect competition, endogenous trade network formation, and the open-ended co-evolution of individual behaviors and economic institutions, to complement existing methods.

6.1 ACE Research Areas

Tesfatsion (2001) classifies the topics recently addressed in ACE research into eight research areas: (i) learning and the embodied mind; (ii) evolution of behavioral norms; (iii) bottom-up modeling of market processes; (iv) formation of economic networks; (v) modeling of organizations; (vi) design of computational agents for automated markets; (vii) parallel experiments with real and computational agents; and (viii) building ACE computational laboratories.

6.1.1 Learning and the Embodied Mind

ACE researchers use a broad range of algorithms to represent the learning processes of computational agents. These algorithms were mainly originally developed with optimality objectives in mind, so that they must be used cautiously for social processes. For automated economic processes, it is appropriate to use learning algorithms based on optimality criteria in which the current strategies of the computational agents jointly co-evolve on the basis of some type of exogenous fitness criterion (e.g., market efficiency). However, in ACE for real-world economic processes with human participants the learning algorithms have to incorporate actual human objectives and decision-making behavior. So, for example, different "neighborhoods" of agents (e.g., firms within different industries), separately co-evolve their strategies on the basis of some type of endogenous fitness criterion (e.g., relative firm profitability).

Due to the numerous differences discovered in laboratory experiments, between actual human-subject behavior and the behavior predicted by traditional rational-agent theories, there is a need for a better modeling of agent behavior. In this respect an embodied-mind approach has been recommended. This approach views games as strategic interaction problems, embedded in natural and social processes. ACE researchers are increasingly moving away from standard off-the-shelf learning algorithms and towards a more systematic investigation of the performance of learning algorithms in various economic decision contexts, in which genetic algorithms are used to implement the evolution of individual strategies.

6.1.2 Evolution of Behavioral Norms

A norm exists in a given social setting if individuals act in a certain way and are punished when they deviate from the norm. The existence of norms may be a matter of degree, and permits one to study the growth and decay of norms as an evolutionary process. Using agent-based computational experiments, mutual cooperation can evolve among self-interested, unrelated agents through reciprocity with little or no explicit forward-looking behavior on the part of the agents. This idea has encouraged the consideration of bounded rationality and evolutionary dynamics. Using agent-based, computational experiments research has shown that various collective behaviors might arise from the interactions of agents following simple rules of behavior.

6.1.3 Bottom-Up Modeling of Market Processes

One of the most active areas of ACE research is the study of the self-organizing capabilities of market processes. Specifically, in an ACE model of oligopolistic markets, globally optimal joint profit maximization pricing across firms results without any explicit price collusion. This type of bottom-up evolution-of-cooperation outcome was new to many economists. Firms were co-evolving their strategies in an intricate structure of path-dependent interactions. Chance and particular interaction histories for a firm mattered for the determination of the final outcomes.

Several specific types of market have been investigated with ACE: financial; electricity; labor; retail; business-to-business; natural resource; entertainment; and automated Internet exchange systems.

Conventional models of financial markets, based on assumptions of rational choice and market efficiency, have not been capable of explaining common empirical patterns such as fat-tailed asset return distributions, high trading volumes, price bubbles, persistence and clustering in asset return volatility, and cross correlations between asset returns, trading volume, and volatility. Due to these difficulties, financial markets have become one of the most active research areas for ACE modelers. ACE financial market models that allow agents to form expectations inductively, using a genetic-fuzzy classifier system, have been able to provide possible explanations for a variety of observed regularities in financial data.

Conventional models of *foreign exchange markets* have performed poorly in explaining exchange rate dynamics. ACE modeling of foreign exchange markets has provided a possible explanation for three empirical stylized facts: peaked and fat-tailed rate change distributions; a negative correlation between trading volume and exchange rate volatility; and a "contrary opinions" phenomenon in which convergence of opinion causes a predicted event to fail to materialize.

Social learning in the form of imitation of strategies is an important factor in *stock markets*, along with individual learning. However, standard stock market models do not include the mechanisms by which such social learning actually takes place. One key finding from ACE research is that market behavior never settles down; initially successful forecasting models quickly become obsolete as soon as they are adopted by increasing numbers of agents. Another key finding is that individual traders do not act as if they believe in the efficient market hypothesis, even though aggregate market statistics suggest that the stock market is efficient.

An ACE framework for energy markets has studied how prices for bulk electricity would be affected by a government-proposed change from a uniform-price auction *to* a discriminatory-price auction. Under a uniform-price auction, all trades occur at the same price, while a discriminatory auction allows different prices for different units, as a function of bid and ask prices submitted. The market is modeled as a sequential game among electricity generators (sellers) with market share and profit objectives. In each trading period each generator submits a supply function expressing its quantity offered at various prices. A key finding is that, when supply function offers are not publicly available, the proposed change from a uniform-price to a discriminatory-price auction permits larger generators to increase their profits relative to smaller generators. Under the discriminatory auction larger generators have a significant informational advantage over smaller generators because they submit more offers and therefore can learn more precisely about the current state of the market. The uniform-price auction mitigates this advantage by letting smaller generators share in the industry's collective learning, by receiving the same market price for their electricity as any other generator.

6.1.4 Formation of Economic Networks

In imperfectly competitive markets with strategically interacting agents it is important to know the manner in which agents determine their transaction partners, because this affects the form of the transaction networks that emerge. Transaction networks are now frequently analyzed by means of transaction cost economics (Williamson 1972), but without emphasizing the dynamics of learning, adaptation, and innovation, nor the development of trust. At the moment, small-world transaction networks, characterized by a relatively well-connected set of neighbor nodes and by short-cut connections with a small average minimum path length between nodes, are attracting increased attention. Such networks have both local connectivity and global reach. An ACE model of a bilateral exchange economy has explored the consequences of restricting trade to small-world trade networks. A key finding is that small-world trade networks provide most of the market-efficiency advantages of the completely connected trade networks, while retaining almost all of the transaction cost economies of the locally connected trade networks.

More recent ACE research on the endogenous formation of trade networks has tended to focus on labor markets. An ACE labor market framework studies the relationship between market structure, worker-employer interaction networks, worksite behaviors, and welfare outcomes. A key finding is that holding job capacity (total potential job openings to total potential work offers) fixed, changes in job concentration (number of workers to number of employers) have only small and unsystematic effects on the market power levels attained.

6.1.5 Modeling of Organizations

A group of people constitutes an *organization* if the group has an objective or performance criterion that transcends the objectives of the individuals within the group. Organizations are viewed as complex adaptive systems themselves. Studies of firms in organization theory have tended to stress the effects of a firm's organizational structure on its own resulting behavior. In contrast, ACE market studies stress the effects of particular types of firm behavioral rules on price dynamics, growth, and market structure. An interesting new direction is combining these two perspectives. A stylized ACE market model may explore how the structure of the market and the internal organization of each participant firm affect the form of the optimal behavioral rules for the participant firms.

More concretely, a firm may choose whether to produce an existing product variety or to introduce a new product variety. The demand for each product variety dies out after a stochastically determined amount of time, so that each firm must engage to some degree in innovation in order to sustain its profitability. Firms differ in their ability to imitate existing product varieties and in their ability to design new product varieties. The differences are due to learning-by-doing effects, as well as to random factors, which alter the organizational structure of each firm. Each firm has an innovation rule determining its choice to innovate or not, and the firms co-evolve these rules over time on the basis of anticipated profitability. Experiments explore how the innovation rule of a firm should adapt both to the structure of the industry as a whole and to the organizational structure of the individual firms to maximize profit.

6.1.6 Design of Computational Agents for Automated Markets

In certain applications, automated contracting through computational agents can increase search efficiency. That is, computational agents are often more effective at finding beneficial contractual arrangements in market contexts with strategically complex multi-agent settings, and with large strategy domains. Therefore, many researchers are now involved in the design of computational agents for automated markets. To date, much of this work has focused on implementation, enforcement, and security issues. In general, the contracts used in automated markets have been binding and these contracts limit the ability of the computational agents to react to unforeseen events.

The recently developed "leveled commitment contract" permits agents to renounce contracts by paying a monetary penalty to the contracting partner, but the efficiency of the resulting contracts depends heavily on the structure of the penalties. Four types of penalties have been considered: (i) fixed; (ii) percentage of contract price; (iii) increasing penalty based on contract start date; and (iv), increasing penalty based on contract breach date. The main finding is that choosing relatively low but positive penalties of breach of contract work best. Surprisingly, however, it has also been found that self-interested myopic agents achieve a higher social welfare level, and more rapidly, than cooperative myopic agents when decommitment penalties are low.

The use of computational agents in automated auction markets on the Internet is growing. The greater search efficiency of computational agents in automated markets may mean that they will displace humans in such tasks. It appears that human bidders in auction experiments who bid against computational bidding agents are consistently outperformed. Hence, the information economy may become the largest multi-agent economic system ever envisioned, comprising billions of adaptive strategically-interacting computational agents.

6.1.7 Parallel Experiments with Real and Computational Agents

Experimentation with human subjects has become an important economic research methodology, but one problem it has, is that it is not possible to know exactly why a human subject is making a particular choice. Rather, the human subject's beliefs and preferences must be inferred from his choices. These may include errors in actions, so that choices might differ from those that the human subject intended to make. In contrast, in ACE experiments with computational agents, the modeler sets the initial conditions of the experiment. As the computational agents then co-evolve their behavioral rules over time, the modeler can attempt to trace this evolution back to its root causes.

There is a potential synergetic role for parallel human subject and computational agent experiments. Human-subject behavior can be used to guide the specification of the behavioral rules that computational agents use. Conversely, computational-agent behavior can be used to formulate hypotheses about the root causes of observed human-subject behaviors.

6.1.8 Building ACE Computational Laboratories

Taking advantage of the recent advent of powerful computational tools, the use of agent- based computational models has been advocated for the testing of economic theories. For example, Nobel laureate Lucas (1987) writes: "(A theory) is not a collection of assertions about the behavior of the actual economy but rather an explicit set of instructions for building a parallel or analog system—a mechanical, imitation economy". However, many economists lack the strong programming skills required for ACE research. Easily learned languages are not powerful enough for many economic applications. General programming languages such as C++ and Java and authoring tools such as AgentSheets, Ascape, RePast, and Swarm provide useful repositories of software for constructing agent-based model economies, but their main appeal is to experienced programmers.

A computational laboratory (CL) provides a potentially useful middle way to avoid these difficulties. ACL is a computational framework that permits the study of systems of multiple interacting agents with controlled and replicable experiments. In particular, a CL with a clear and easily manipulated graphical user interface can be used to test the sensitivity of a system to changes in a wide variety of key parameters without the need to do any original programming. For example, a CL has been designed specifically for the study of trade network formation in a variety of market contexts. This *Trade Network Game* (*TNG*) *Lab* comprises buyers, sellers, and dealers who repeatedly search for preferred trade partners, engage in risky trades modeled as non-cooperative games, and evolve their trade strategies over time. The evolution of trade networks is visualized dynamically by means of real-time animations and real-time performance chart displays. This example may encourage the routine construction and use of CLs for social sciences.

6.2 Criticism Against ACE

Although many economists are dissatisfied with conventional economic models, they have also serious doubts about ACE. This is natural since any novel methodology a paradigm will be challenged and scrutinized before it is accepted.

First, critics point out that computational methods produce only examples, whereas conventional economic theory aims to produce theorems, which apply in any economy satisfying the assumptions of the theorems. Some theorems in economics, such as existence theorems in general equilibrium or game theory, will cover an infinite number of possible cases. However, the substantive gap between "examples" and "theorem" is less clear.

Theories usually characterize a class of examples but, in order to attain analytical tractability, many interesting phenomena may be missed. Computations examine a finite set of examples, but these are taken from a much more robust set of possible specifications. This allows more flexible functional form specifications as well as more complex and realistic assumptions. The relevance and robustness of examples is more important than the number of examples, and computational methods allow one to examine cases that theory cannot touch. Furthermore, computation can often give us insights when there are no general theorems.

Second, critics point out that numerical results in computational work have errors. However, careful numerical work can reduce numerical errors. Theoretical models may not have errors when they solve particular cases, but they often commit specification errors by focusing on tractable cases. In this respect, computational work has an advantage because numerical errors can be reduced through computation. The issue is not whether there are errors, but where those errors are, and how crucial they are. The key fact is that economists face a trade-off between the numerical errors in computational work and oversimplifying assumptions in analytically tractable models. As Tukey (1962) put it, "Far better an approximate answer to the right question… than an exact answer to the wrong question…".

Third, critics argue that computational models are black boxes that offer few if any insights. A single example with many factors contributing to the result may show what is possible, but one example cannot sort out the relative importance of a model's various components. It is unclear how much can be inferred from a few examples. A few examples may not demonstrate much, but a few thousand well chosen examples can be more convincing, and a few million examples may be as compelling as any theorem.

6.3 Open Issues for ACE Research

A key open issue for ACE research area (i) *learning and the embodied mind*— is how to model the minds of the computational agents. Should these minds be viewed according to traditional artificial intelligence terms, as logical machines with added data filing cabinets? Or should they instead be viewed as observers of embodied activity. For the design of a fully automated market, the minds of computational agents should not have to imitate those of real people. This could be detrimental to good market performance. On the other hand, if the focus is on the modeling of some real-world economic processes with human participants, then similarity might be essential to ensure predictive power.

Another issue is with what degree of flexibility should agent learning in ACE frameworks be specified? ACE studies tend to rely on learning algorithms in the form of relatively simple updating equations with fixed parameterizations. However, the evidence on these algorithms strongly suggests that no one algorithm performs best in all situations. Nor does any one algorithm match best to observed human decision-making behavior under all conditions. A better way to proceed is to permit the ACE agents to learn to learn. For example, each agent could be permitted to evolve a repertoire of behavioral rules or modes which the agent selectively activates depending on the situation at hand.

An important issue for ACE research area (ii) *the evolution of behavioral norms*—is how mutual cooperation evolves among economic agents even when cheating reaps immediate gains and binding commitments are not possible. What roles do reputation, trust, reciprocity, retaliation, spitefulness, and punishment play? More generally, how do exchange customs and other behavioral norms for economic processes come to be established, and how stable are these norms over time? Are these behavioral norms diffusing across traditional political and cultural boundaries, resulting in an increasingly homogeneous global economy?

The evolution of behavioral norms has also been studied in classical game theory, which explains this evolution on the basis of strategic considerations, such as instrumental cooperation in anticipation of future reciprocity. In contrast, ACE research places equal or greater stress on peer emulation, parental imitation, and other socialization forces which underlie the transmission of culture.

A fruitful area for future ACE research is the evolution of behavioral norms in collective action situations, such as the collective usage of common-pool resources. The factors that can make these problems so challenging for standard economic modeling—e.g., face-to-face communication, trust, and peer pressure—can be modeled within an ACE framework.

A challenge for ACE research area (iii) *the bottom-up modeling of markets*—is how to explain the evolution of markets and other market-related economic institutions. Much ACE research focuses on the evolution of "horizontal" institutional structures, e.g., trade networks and monetary exchange systems. However, real-world economies are strongly hierarchical and hierarchies are essential to help individuals sort information in a complex world.

The question driving ACE research area (iv) *the formation of economic networks*—is the manner in which economic interaction networks are determined through the deliberate choice of partners as well as by chance. An interaction might consist of some kind of game situation in which partners choose actions strategically, so that the payoff that results from any given choice of partner might not be knowable in advance. This leads to a complicated feedback process in which current partner choices are influenced by past action choices and current action choices are influenced by past partner choices.

The main questions in research area (v) *the modeling of organizations*—have largely been normative. What is the optimal organizational structure for achieving an organization's goals? More generally, what is the relationship between environmental properties, organizational structure, and organizational performance? The increased use of ACE modeling in this research area may permit a quantitative study of organizations within broader economic settings, e.g., the study of intra-firm organization for multiple firms participating within a market.

One focus of research area (vi) *the design of computational agents for automated markets*, is the extent to which interaction networks are important for predicting market outcomes. If interaction effects are weak, as in some types of auction markets, then the structural aspects of the market (e.g., numbers of buyers and sellers, costs, capacities) will be the primary determinants of market outcomes. In this case, each different market structure should map into a relatively simple central-tendency output distribution in response to varying structural conditions. If interaction effects are strong, as in labor markets, then each different market structure might map into a spectral distribution of possible market outcomes, which may be clustered around two or more distinct "attractors" corresponding to distinct possible interaction networks. Moreover, strong interaction effects might also increase the speed of convergence to these attractors in highly connected networks and impede or inhibit convergence, if networks are sparsely connected or disconnected.

A few challenging issues exist for ACE research area (vii) *parallel experiments with real and computational agents*, such as the need to make the parallel experiments truly parallel, so that comparisons are meaningful and lead to robust insights. One major hurdle is the need to capture the crucial aspects of an experimental design as perceived by human participants in the initial conditions of the ACE. However, this can be hard to achieve, because the perceptions of human participants in an experiment can differ systematically from the perceptions of the investigator. Asking experimental subjects what they were trying to do in an experiment tends not to yield reliable data, since participants may try to rationalize their previous actions with post hoc explanations, or try to give responses that they believe would please the experimenter. Furthermore, experiments with human participants generally have to be kept short and simple to prevent boredom or fatigue among the participants and to keep them within the budgetary constraints of the investigators, since human subjects in economic experiments must be paid. In contrast, computational agents face no such limitations.

A prime issue for ACE area (viii) *building ACE computational laboratories*— is methodological. This is the need to construct computational laboratories (CLs) that permit the rigorous study of complex distributed multi-agent systems through controlled experimentation. Should a separate CL be constructed for each application, or should researchers strive for general multi-purpose platforms? How can experimental findings be effectively communicated to other researchers by means of descriptive statistics and graphical visualizations without information overload? How might these findings be validated by comparisons with data obtained from other sources?

A particularly important unresolved issue for area (viii) is the need to ensure that findings from ACE experiments are robust in that they reflect fundamental aspects of an economic application and not simply the peculiarities of the particular hardware or software used to implement the experiments. A particular language should ensure independence of the hardware platform, but not independence of specific software implementation features. In this respect a possible approach is model docking, the alignment of different computational models to enable them to model the same application problem. Regardless of the approach taken, however, an essential prerequisite is that the source code must be openly disseminated to other researchers for replication purposes.

Parameter choice is important in ACE modeling. The scale and the *time horizons* assumed in ACE modeling are crucial. The ACE studies illustrated above might be classified as intermediate-run studies, in that they focus on evolutionary processes taking place over many, but not infinitely many, time periods. Some research is focused on the probability with which different kinds of behavioral norms and institutions emerge in the very long run. ACE models cannot be used directly to confirm or reject the long-run distributional predictions of these studies. However, ACE models could be used for testing for speeds of convergence in some cases.

Finally, does ACE have anything to say about the *direction of causality* between individuals and social groupings? ACE does permit causality to be established in many cases, because parameters of the economy can be varied exogenously and their effects measured. This has allowed researchers to conclude that the answer to the question "which must come first, individuals or social groupings," is "neither". Rather, it depends on details of how the economy is specified. As in the real world, individuals and social groupings co-evolve together in an intricate dance through time, and the dynamics of the dance depends on many details. ACE research is only just beginning to model this complex two-way feedback process.

6.4 Potential Costs and Benefits

ACE model economies are grounded in the interactions of autonomous adaptive agents, broadly defined to include economic, social, and environmental entities. ACE agents are necessarily constrained by the initial conditions set by the modeler. However, the dynamics of the ensuing economic process are micro founded in that they are governed by agent-agent interactions. The state of the economy at each point in time is given by the internal attributes of the individual agents that currently populate the economy. This type of dynamical description should have direct attractiveness for economists and other social scientists and increase the transparency and clarity of the modeling process.

A growing body of computational evidence suggests that simple individual behaviors can generate complex macro regularities. If this evidence receives empirical support, further improvements in explanatory clarity can be expected from ACE modeling.

The use of ACE model economies could also facilitate the development and testing of integrated theories in many different fields of social science. In particular, ACE frameworks could encourage economists to address growth, distribution, and welfare issues in a more comprehensive manner embracing a variety of economic, social, political, and psychological factors.

Moreover, ACE model economies can be used to test economic theories developed using more standard modeling approaches. By testing, we mean that we study whether the theory makes accurate predictions in an economy in which a model can be applied. This typically is an economy in which not all assumptions of the model are satisfied (if all assumptions of a model are satisfied, than by pure logic, a formally derived theory must be true). ACE models can also be used to test the robustness of these theories to relaxations of their standard assumptions, such as common knowledge of rationality, selfish preferences, rational expectations, and perfect capital markets. Finally, ACE model economies can be used to test for the possibility that multiple distinct microstructures are capable of supporting a given macro regularity.

7 The Economics of Artificial Intelligence

7.1 Implications of AI for Economic Theory: Back to the Future

In many respects, the advent of artificial intelligence promises to be a bonanza for classical economic theory. In classical models, agents are assumed to be fully rational in the sense that, given their objectives, they have no computational limits in making the best decisions to achieve them. This ability will be the defining characteristic of intelligent artificial agents.

Economic theory is intended to provide an account of how humans behave. Experimental evidence has exposed the limits of humans' computational abilities, and shown that these limits are binding in many common types of economic decisions. Thus, among some economists, classical models are thought to describe only highly sophisticated actors such as central banks or large firms, or alternatively to represent normative models of how an economic agent should act. Behavioral economic models, which allow individuals to make boundedly rational decisions, have become fashionable as descriptive models of how humans make decisions.

However, for artificially intelligent agents, with essentially no limits of computational power, classical theory becomes relevant as a description of behavior. In the domain of individual choice, artificial agents can use objective probabilities rather than distorting them. They can discount the future exponentially rather than hyperbolically or time-inconsistently. They can have expectations of the future that are unbiased given the information they have available, rather than extrapolating from previous trends.

Furthermore, in interactive settings, classical game theory would be relevant. Game theory requires very strong assumptions both on the objectives and reasoning ability of an individual and on his beliefs about the objectives and reasoning ability of those with whom she interacts. Suppose a hyper-rational AI knows that she is interacting with similar agents. Furthermore, suppose that the rationality of agents is common knowledge. This means that classical game theory should apply and that Nash equilibrium is an appropriate model to describe the outcome of their interaction.

In classical dynamic models of savings and economic growth, agents were assumed to be infinitely lived. For example, in the well-known Ramsey (1928) savings model, which served as the basis for the subsequent literature on optimal economic growth, an infinitely lived agent chooses a time-path of consumption and savings to maximize his utility over an infinite time horizon. The infinite horizon assumption was viewed as a convenient analytical device that made the appropriate optimization problem solvable. However, the advent of Methuselarity promises to make infinite horizon models descriptive.

Established models of endogenous growth, such as those of Lucas (1986) and Romer (1990) can describe how a singularity might be achieved. In Lucas' model, there is a production process in the economy, which uses labor, capital and human capital, as inputs. Human capital represents productivity-enhancing human experience and skills that result from prior investment in education and learning on the job. In his model, labor and capital display diminishing returns, but human capital yields increasing returns. That is, more investment in human capital increases production at an increasing rate, and the economy can asymptotically approach singularity. An implication is that, if human capital is interpreted as the knowledge base possessed by artificially intelligent agents, then the model captures how artificial intelligence can lead to a singularity.

In Romer's model, productivity is a function of the number of people in the economy. The greater the number of people, the more productive is the economy. The intuition is that the greater the number of agents, the more productivity-enhancing ideas that they can generate. However, each idea benefits all members of the economy. Thus, as the number of individuals in the economy becomes arbitrarily large, the economy's growth rate approaches infinity. The model can be interpreted as describing an economy populated with artificially intelligent agents, each of whom are potentially capable of inventing technologies that enhance productivity. If an arbitrarily large number of artificially intelligent agents can be produced, each of whom might come up with useful ideas, the economy would accelerate to approach an infinite growth rate.

Economic theory also provides a framework to consider the implications of friendly and unfriendly Artificial Intelligence. Individuals are assumed to maximize a utility function. This is a function that represents their preferences, in the sense that it takes on greater values for more preferred outcomes. The classical economic approach assumes that an individual's utility consists of only her own payoffs, which correspond to the objectives of the *indifferent* AI agents described earlier. However, any number of social preference elements can be added to the utility function. Humans have been shown in experimental studies to exhibit altruism, a preference to increase the payoffs of others if they feel these others have too little. They also often have social welfare preferences, a willingness to sacrifice their own interests for the sake of the group, in some cases. They are also willing to repay kind actions of others, which is referred to as positive reciprocity. Economic theory can incorporate these elements into the utility function and predict the behavior of Friendly AI in different types of interaction. It can similarly model unfriendly AI, and thus can potentially model how constraints can be designed to keep unfriendly agents in check. This analysis can use the tools of mechanism design (Hurwicz 1973), a branch of game theory.

7.2 Economic History and the Singularity

Historical growth rates, rather than following a smooth accelerating trend over time have tended to be roughly piecewise linear. In other words, growth is more or less constant over a long period of time but punctuated with abrupt, seemingly unheralded transitions from one economic era to another. Each of these transitions is marked by a sudden and drastic increase in the rate of economic growth.

Within each economic era the question of whether growth speeds up or slows down depends on two competing factors. Deceleration typically results as innovators exhaust the easy ideas—the low-hanging fruit. But acceleration also follows as the economy, by getting larger, enables its members to explore an ever-increasing number of innovations.

The economic historian Angus Maddison argues that that between 1950 and 2003, world GDP growth was relatively steady. During that time, despite enormous technical change, no particular technology left much of a fingerprint on the data, and no short-term accelerations in growth could be attributed to a particular technological development. Therefore, Maddison's data offer little support for the idea that innovation and growth have accelerated recently.

However, the data give a different conclusion if taken over a longer time horizon. Bradford DeLong considers world output over the last 7,000 years. For most of that time, growth proceeded at a relatively steady exponential rate, with a doubling of output about every 900 years. But within the past few centuries, something dramatic happened: output began doubling faster and faster, approaching a new steady doubling time of about 15 years. That's about 60 times as fast as it had been in the previous seven millennia.

In the roughly 2 million years that our ancestors lived as hunters and gatherers, the population rose from about 10,000 proto-humans (primitive ancestors of modern humans who began to walk upright) to about 4 million modern humans. This implies that if the growth pattern during this era was fairly steady, then on average the population must have doubled about every quarter million years. Beginning about 10,000 years ago, when humans began to settle down and live as farmers, the farming population doubled about every 900 years–some 250 times as fast as before.

Hanson (2008) suggests that there are perhaps five eras during which growth has exhibited a sharp positive increase: the universe after the Big Bang, the emergence of the human brain, the appearance of the hunting economy, the advent of the farming economy, and later of the industrial economy. Each new era was characterized by a growth rate that was between 60 and 250 times as fast as that of the previous era. Each switch was completed in much less time than the previous one. These switches can be viewed as Singularities.

He presents a long term summary of life, the universe and everything which goes as follows. The universe started fourteen billion years ago, life appeared by four billion years ago, and on Earth animals started growing larger and smarter about half a billion years ago. Humans appeared a few million years ago, farming started about ten thousand years ago, industry started about two hundred years ago, and computers started a few decades ago.

According to Hanson's calculations, history is a sequence of faster and faster exponential growth modes. First the largest animal brains grew slowly, and then the wealth of human hunters grew faster. Next farmer wealth grew much faster, and finally industry wealth grew faster still. Perhaps each new growth mode could not start until the previous mode had reached a certain enabling scale. Humans could not grow via culture until animal brains were large enough, farming was not feasible until hunters were dense enough, and industry was not possible until there are enough farmers near each other.

While growth rates have varied widely, growth rate changes have been surprisingly consistent—each mode exhibited growth between one hundred and fifty to three hundred times faster than its predecessor. Also, the recent modes have made a similar number of doublings before giving rise to a new mode.

The singularities are the result of critical innovations. Most innovations happen within a given growth era and do not change its basic growth rate. A few exceedingly rare innovations, however, do suddenly change everything. Agriculture was one such innovation; industry was another.

According to Hanson, another Singularity could lie just ahead. Data on the previous singularities might form a guide to what such a transition might look like if previous dynamics continue to apply. If a new transition were to show the same pattern as the effect of agriculture and industrialization, then growth would quickly speed up by between 60 and 250-fold. If we extrapolate from previous historical patterns, the world economy, which now doubles in size every 15 years or so, would soon double in somewhere between a week or a month after the next critical transition.

What innovation could induce sudden acceleration in economic growth? No improvement within just one small sector of the economy could do the trick. In advanced countries today, farming, mining, energy, communications, transportation, and construction each account for only a small percentage of economic activity. Innovations with specific application in only one of these areas, even if it greatly enhanced productivity in that sector, would provide at best a small increase in overall output. Even drastic advances in nanotechnology would do no more than merely lower the cost of capital for manufacturing, which now makes up less than 10 % of U.S. GDP.

However, the next radical jump in economic growth may come from something that has a profound effect on everything, because it addresses the one permanent shortage in our entire economy: human time. About two thirds of all income in the rich countries is paid directly as wages and any innovation that could replace or dramatically improve the efficiency of human labor would be a very big deal. Greatly lowering this cost could have a huge impact. And a robotics or artificial intelligence technology which may substitute on a large scale for most human labor may greatly lower labor costs. One of the pillars of the modern Singularity hypothesis is that very intelligent machines will produce the next Singularity.

7.3 Economics of Human–Machine Interaction

Friedman (2011) has investigated the economics of the introduction of new technologies on product and on labor markets. In general, recent and influential new technologies, such as computer software and nanotechnology, are characterized by a distinctive cost structure. They have very high fixed costs of research and development, and of launching initial production. However, the marginal cost of producing additional units is very low. The production of new AI systems, including autonomous robots, can be expected to generally have this type of cost structure.

For the first in a new class of products, a natural monopoly may briefly exist. Depending on how well a patent regime can be enforced, and experience suggests that this will be very difficult at the global level, new firms will be able to enter after some time. If these firms make products which are close but not perfect substitutes, a situation of monopolistic competition would prevail. Because of the cost structure, two firms making an identical product would not be able to co-exist, so an entrant with a cheaper or better version of the same product can rapidly completely wipe out an incumbent.

The arrival of AI will greatly influence the labor market. Augmentations of humans that increase their productivity will also increase their wages. Inequality between those humans who are augmented and those who are not can be expected to increase.

The introduction of autonomous AI workers on the labor market will have profound effects. This will cause a much larger upheaval on the market than that caused by the introduction of China and India into the world economy over the last two decades. However, history has witnessed even more drastic technological shocks to the labor market and emerged more prosperous. In Western countries, until 250 years ago, farming was the dominant occupation, employing perhaps 95 % of the labor force. This share has declined to roughly 2 %. This enormous upheaval was wrought by the industrial revolution. Humanity survived and prospered.

Indeed, many kinds of labor have already been replaced by machines. At first, machines replaced humans at tasks needing physical strength, but more recently machines have replaced humans at mental tasks. If a huge number of important tasks formerly in the human realm were now achievable with machines, the economy could start growing much faster, for three reasons. First, capable machines could be created in much less time than it takes to breed, rear, and educate new human workers. Second, the cost of computing has long been falling much faster than the growth of the economy. When the workforce is largely composed of computers, the cost of making computer workers will therefore fall at that faster rate, with all that this entails for economic growth. Third, as the economy begins growing faster, computer usage and the resources devoted to developing computers will also grow faster. And because innovation is faster when more people use and study something, computer performance may be expected to improve even faster than in the past.

However, this should not make human workers as a whole worse off, though workers in some occupations will suffer. First of all, all humans can be expected to benefit enormously from the lower prices that the expected gains in efficiency will create. Economic theory predicts that the mix of human and machine would follow the Law of Comparative Advantage. This is a principle, usually applied at the level of countries engaged in international trade. Countries export, and may under some conditions fully specialize, in those products which they produce relatively efficiently compared to other products. This has the implication that every country exports some products. This is true even for those countries that are less efficient producing every product than another country.

The same would apply to the labor of man and machines. Even if machines eventually become more efficient at every economically valuable task than humans, humans would still be employed in those sectors, in which their disadvantage in smallest. The resource that is human labor would not go undemanded. For example, suppose that machines are 50 times more efficient than humans at preparing food but only 5 times as efficient at dentistry; then humans willing to work will continue to find employment as dentists.

Human wages will depend on the particular sector and tasks they perform. When humans and machines are substitutes, and machines can be produced at very low cost, human wages in that sector can be expected to fall as demand for them decreases. On the other hand, for tasks where humans and machines are complements, demand for human labor would rise, which would tend to increase wages. However, the wage changes would be mitigated by workers moving away from sectors in which humans and machines are substitutes into sectors in which they are complements. Furthermore, there might still be some human tasks left where machines are not demanded despite their efficiency. For example, some rich people, for reasons of taste or status, might still want to be served and entertained by real human beings and for such jobs, human wages could rise.

What about machine wages? Eventually it will become very cheap to produce new AI workers as well as to take them out of the labor force. Whether AI workers are the property of their creators, or are working for their own benefit, a principle termed the Iron Law of Wages, originally proposed by Ferdinand Lasalle, would seem to apply. The Iron Law of Wages states that the price of labor seeks a level that is near its subsistence level. For robot workers, this would be at the marginal cost of their operation, which would primarily consist of the costs of power, replacement parts, and maintenance. If wages were greater than this level, it would mean that new machines could be profitably introduced into the market, bidding down wages. If wages were lower than marginal cost, it would mean that machines would be withdrawn from the labor force until the break-even point is reached.

7.4 Methuselarity and Economic Behavior

Methuslarity will change many current patterns of economic behavior. The current human lifecycle can be thought of as consisting of three stages. During the first stage, childhood and adolescence, individuals invest in skills to be used in the future. During the second stage, working life, they supply labor and earn income. Some of this income is used for consumption, some used to pay back debt incurred early in life, and some used to save for retirement. The third stage is retirement, in which the individual consumes part or all of her savings, leaving the remainder to heirs.

The advent of very long healthy lives with low morbidity will likely more or less eliminate the third stage. Without age-related illnesses, most deaths will be caused by accidents or catastrophic events, and not be preceded by a period of infirmity. Instead of retirement, taking long breaks between spells of work may become more common, and some savings will be accumulated for these periods, and for bequests should sudden death occur. However, individuals would typically no longer save for retirement, a permanent period of leisure when one expects never to return to work. The first phase would become longer, as people will invest more in themselves because they have longer to reap the rewards. Multiple careers would become more common.

Kotlikoff (1979) analyses the implications of large life-extension. It would have the effect of shifting an individual's budget constraint outward, since there would be more scope for intertemporal substitution of consumption. Life extension would increase the ratio of productive to unproductive persons, and increase the intensity of capital of the economy. All of these changes should make the world richer, and would mean acceleration in the economic gains that previous increases of life expectancy have yielded. Murphy and Topel (2006) estimate that from 1970 to 2000, gains in life expectancy added about $3.2 trillion per year to national wealth in the US alone. A number of studies find that a five year increase in life expectancy adds between 0.1 and 0.6 % to a nation's annual growth rate (see Bloom et al. 2008).

Methuselarity would also affect politics greatly, and intergenerational relations would be affected. Politically difficult decisions would have to be made to increase the pensionable age and change health care benefits for the elderly. The problem would be exacerbated by the likelihood that there would be, at least initially, great inequality in lifespans. Wealthy individuals would be the most likely to receive life-extending treatments first, and therefore current pension systems may become severely regressive. This would likely provoke demands for reform.

8 State of the Art and Challenges for AGI

The earlier discussion of different approaches to AGI suggests that the integration of several of the approaches into a single AGI research agenda might be desirable. By far the most intensely integrative AGI approach is the *Novamente* AI approach (Goerzel 2007). The Novamente AI Engine is in part an original system and in part an integration of ideas from prior work on narrow AI and AGI. The Novamente design is unique in its overall architecture and incorporates aspects of many previous AI paradigms such as genetic programming, neural networks, agent systems, evolutionary programming, reinforcement learning, and probabilistic reasoning.

The principles underlying the Novamente design have been derived from a novel complex-systems-based theory of mind called the *psynet model.* The psynet model lays out a series of properties that must be fulfilled by any software system if it is going to be an autonomous, self-organizing, self-evolving system, with its own understanding of the world, and the ability to relate to humans on a mind-to-mind rather than a software-program-to-mind level. At the moment, a complete Novamente design has been laid out in detail, but implementation is not yet complete. The end result will be an autonomous AGI system, oriented toward assisting humans in collectively solving pragmatic problems.

Eventually, AGI's will have many significant advantages over biological intelligences. The ability to modify their own underlying structures and dynamics, will give AGI the capacity for self-improvement vastly exceeding that possessed by humans. AGI designs based too closely on the human brain may not be able to exploit the unique advantages available to digital intelligences.

Increases in computational power and the emergence of technologies like Grid computing also contribute to a positive outlook for AGI. While it is possible that, in the not too distant future, regular desktop machines will be able to run AGI software comfortably, today's AGI prototypes are extremely resource intensive, and the growing availability of world-wide computing farms would greatly benefit AGI research.

Traditional, narrow AI is very valuable, but AGI research is a very present and viable option. The complementary and related fields are mature enough, the computing power is becoming increasingly easier and cheaper to obtain, and AGI itself is ready for popularization.

Optimistic observers expect the following achievements in the realm of AI in upcoming years:

- The tipping point of human life expectancy will be reached, with every year of research guaranteeing at least one more year of life expectancy. In contrast, in 2007, 3–4 months of life expectancy were added due to the development of new medicines and treatments.
- The world energy crisis will be resolved once cheap, high-efficiency solar panels can be synthesized by nano-machines and produced for mass use.
- In 2019, a $1,000 PC will have as much power as the human brain and in 2029 it will be 1,000 times more powerful than the human brain.
- Reverse engineering of the human brain will be completed in 2029.

The next grand challenges for future research appear to be: theoretical understanding of behavior; achieving higher level intelligence; automated design methods (artificial evolution and morphogenesis), and "moving into the real world" (Pfeifer and Iida 2004).

Theoretical Understanding of Behavior

The question is how particular behaviors in the real world can be achieved with artificial agents. This has to do with the "here and now" time scale of the mechanisms behind behavior. There are not yet general purpose perceptual systems and there is still an insufficient understanding of how we can achieve rapid legged locomotion. Although there has been a lot of progress in research on humanoid walking robots, especially in Japan, most of these robots still walk more slowly than humans, and their walking style looks somewhat unnatural. There should be a match in the complexity of the sensory, motor and neural control systems. In this sense many robotic systems are unbalanced. To date, most robots are specialized, either for walking, other types of locomotion, or sensory-motor manipulation. However, rarely are these robots skilled at performing a wide spectrum of tasks. This is due to conceptual and engineering limitations. Huge transdisciplinary efforts between engineering, biomechanics, and material science will be required to make progress here.

Behavior in general requires sensory-motor coordination that in natural systems is achieved by a subtle interplay of morphology (of the sensory and motor systems), materials, control, and interaction with the environment. Little research has been done on quantifying morphology and materials in computational terms. Better materials would almost certainly entail a quantum leap in artificial intelligence. Moreover, there are challenges concerning the various sensory modalities such as in haptics, that is, communication via touching.

Achieving Higher Level Intelligence

Higher level intelligence is not purely sensory-motor. It also refers also to thinking, natural language, emotion, and consciousness. In natural systems, brains are intrinsically intertwined with enacted embodiment, and cannot be clearly separated from it. The question is how organisms can acquire meaning, how they can learn about the real world, and how they can combine what they have learned to generate symbolic behavior, a problem known as the "symbol grounding problem." There is general agreement that learning will make substantial contributions towards a solution. Through the physical interaction with the environment, the agent induces or generates sensory stimulation, which in fact is the enabler of learning as the basis for higher level intelligence.

Machine learning addresses two interrelated problems: the development of software that improves automatically through experience and the extraction of expert rules from a large volume of specific data. Systems capable of exhibiting such characteristics are important because they have the potential to reach higher levels of performance than systems that must be modified manually to deal with situations their designers did not anticipate. Hence, software must be automatically adapted to new or changing users and runtime environments, and to accommodate for the rapidly increasing quantities of diverse data available today.

Automated Design Methods (artificial evolution and morphogenesis)

The question is what are the basic design considerations for creating a synthetic model of the evolution of living systems (i.e. an 'artificial life' system)? Automated methods must be employed because humans will no longer be able to manually design all aspects of such systems. The grand challenge is to develop truly complex creatures capable of communication, language, high-level cognition, and—perhaps—consciousness. The extent to which physically realistic simulations are sufficient for this purpose, and whether evolution actually must happen in the real world with its infinite richness, are deep and currently unanswered issues.

Moving into the Real World

The last grand challenge concerns, very generally speaking, the "move into the real world." Enacted embodied artificial intelligence is based on the idea that true intelligence always requires interaction with the real world. Building intelligent robots that are capable of performing a wide range of tasks remains a grand challenge. *Cyborgs* could be viewed as a way to “move into the real world”. Combining biological neural tissue and a real-world artifact opens up entirely new avenues in man–machine interaction. On the one hand, we may learn something about neural functioning, and on the other we might be able to better understand how to control robots by observing the natural neurons. Medical applications in prosthetics, such as an artificial device replacing a missing body part, are obvious candidates for practical applications.

Finally, a big challenge, conceptually and from an engineering perspective, is the development of systems in the real world of self-repair, self-assembly, and self-reconfiguration.

8.1 The Future of Artificial Intelligence

Well before the end of the 21st century, thinking on non-biological substrates will dominate and biological thinking will be stuck at 1,026 calculations per second. Nanobot technology (nano robots with the size of human blood cells, which can communicate with each other wirelessly) will expand our minds in many ways. Nanobots will be introduced without surgery, likely injecting or swallowing them. They can also be directed to leave the body, so that the process is easily reversible. They can take up trillions of positions throughout the brain.

The electronic circuits in a computer are already more than ten million times faster than a human neuron’s electro-mechanical processes. The combination of human level intelligence with a computer’s inherent superiority in the speed, accuracy, and sharing ability of its memory will be formidable.

Supercomputers should have achieved human brain capacity by 2010 and PCs may do so around 2020. By the second decade of the 21st century, computers will be able to read on their own, understanding and modeling what they have read. Machines will gather knowledge on their own initiative.

By 2030, it will take a village of human brains (around a thousand) to match $1,000 of computing. By 2030 nanobot technology will be viable and brain scanning will be a prominent application. By 2050, $100 of computing will equal the processing power of all the human brains on Earth that would still be using carbon-based neurons.

However, achieving the computational capacity of the human brain with a machine will not automatically produce human levels of capability in some areas. These may include musical and artistic aptitude, creativity, physically moving through the world and understanding and responding appropriately to emotion. The requisite hardware capacity is a necessary, but not a sufficient, condition. The software of intelligence is also critical. Mastering the software of intelligence will take place through reverse engineering the human brain and copying its design. The basic technologies to scan a brain exist today, just not with the requisite speed, cost and size. However, these are improving at a double exponential pace. Nanobot-based scanning will be more practical than scanning the brain from outside.

Objectively, after scanning and re-instating all of the neural details of a specific person into a human-like intelligent entity, the newly emergent "person" will appear to other observers to have very much the same personality, history and memory as the person originally scanned. This new person will have a body enhanced through biotechnology and nanotechnology. The future machines will claim to have spiritual experiences, but ultimately, consciousness cannot objectively be measured. There is no consensus yet about whether nonhuman entities could become conscious.

Subjectively, consciousness of the new entity is critically important: to feel pain, and discomfort, to have own intentions, own free will, to have subjective experiences. If he says: "I am lonely, please keep me company", does that settle the issue? If I am scanned, is this really me? Alas, "the old Me" has to sit back and watch the new "Me" succeed in endeavors that the old Me could only dream about. While this new "Me" is recognizably similar to "the old Me", I still would conclude that "he" is not "Me", because I still exist independently. However, the replacement of my brain with a non-biological equivalent leads into a new Me and may lead to termination the old Me. What appears the continuing existence of just one Me is really the creation of a new Me and the termination of the old Me.

The future of AGI is a big, difficult, complicated issue. No one can sensibly claim to know what is going to happen. However, a few plausible categories of general scenarios are listed here:

1. *Steady Progress Scenario*: incremental progress gradually and slowly becoming less and less narrow in the direction of AGI.
2. *Dead-End Scenario*: narrow AI research continues and leads to various domain specific successes but does not succeed progressively moving toward AGI.
3. *AGI-Based Singularity Scenario*: scientific and technological progress occurs so fast that the rate of advancement is effectively infinite. The knowledge-advancement curve becomes vertical. There is still a dramatic, irreducible uncertainty attached to the development of any future technology as radical as AGI, so that the character of the human condition following such a major change is substantially unknown.
4. Kurzweil Scenario: AGI is achieved via scanning human brains, figuring out the nature of human thought from these scans, and then replicating the human brain function on massively powerful computer hardware.
5. *The Path to Posthumanity Scenario*: the most likely future is one in which human–level AGI is achieved via integrative methods synthesizing insights from computer science, cognitive science and other disciplines inspired by neuroscience rather than via emulation of the human brain. Kurzweil does not provide any proof that an AI-driven Singularity is upon us. In any extrapolation of the future of a complex real-world system there can be no such thing as proof, only at best "probably approximately correct predictions". Kurzweil may be underestimating the uncertainty involved in predicting the future of complex, open systems like human societies. Kurzweil seems to have succumbed to a certain extent to overconfidence. How certain could a date like 2045 for human-level AI possibly be? What is the variance of this estimate? There is a lot more uncertainty in the future than Kurzweil

wants to recognize. A big problem is how to model consciousness and experience. Kurzweil may be too confident in his predictions about the intrinsically unpredictable. Kurzweil extrapolates not from contemporary progress in the AI field, but rather from contemporary progress in computer hardware and brain scanning.

Brain-scanning and computer-hardware will allow effective human brain emulation sometime in the next few decades. A crucial metaphysical question may be how far should devices be developed to promote direct brain–machine interactions, or apply external or internal controls of the body or the brain? Beyond a certain point, what matters most to humans may not be functional things or physical limitations, but relational, moral, spiritual, aesthetic, and creative aspects.

It is not yet clear what sorts of interactions between design and evolution will prove to be most helpful to integrate evolution with AI.AI may be converting more and more of the Earth's matter into engineered, computational substrate capable of supporting more AI's until the whole Earth is one gigantic computer. AI would radiate out into space in all directions from the Earth, breaking down whole planets, moons and meteorites and reassembling them into giant computers. Space technology might become advanced enough to provide the Earth permanent protection from the threat of asteroid impacts. The universe will be wakened up as all the inanimate dumb matter (rocks, dust, gases, etc.) is converted into structured matter capable of supporting life, albeit synthetic life. This process could be complete by 2200 or so, or it might take billions of years, depending on whether or not machines could figure out how to circumvent the speed of light for the purpose of space travel. AI human hybrids, which will become so integrated that they will constitute a new category of life, would have both supreme intelligence and may achieve physical control over the universe.

When computer scientists succeed in developing intelligent machines that can do everything better than humans can, then either of two possibilities might occur.

First, the machines might be permitted to make their own decisions without human oversight. The human race might easily permit itself to become dependent on the machines. As society and the problems that face it become more and more complex and machines become more and more intelligent, people will let machines make more of their decisions for them, because machine-made decisions will bring better results than man-made ones. Then the machines will be in effective control.

Second, human control over the machines might be retained. Then the average man may have control over certain private machines of his own, but control over large systems of machines will be in the hands of an elite which will have greater control over the masses.

Since human work may no longer be necessary, the human masses may become superfluous and exterminated if the elite is ruthless. If the elite is humane, it may use propaganda or other psychological or biological techniques to reduce the birth rate until the mass of humanity becomes extinct.

If the elite consist of more compassionate individuals, they may be good shepherds to the rest of the human race. They will check that everyone's physical needs are satisfied, that all children are raised under hygienic conditions, that everyone has a wholesome hobby to keep him busy, and that anyone who is dissatisfied undergoes treatment to cure his "problem." In such a society, engineered humans may be physically healthy, even happy, but they will certainly not be free. Governments may intervene by passing laws protecting human rights from robots and requiring robots to be benevolent.

The most compelling 21st-century technologies—genetic engineering, nanotechnology and robotics (GNR)—pose a different threat than the technologies that have come before. Robots, engineered organisms, and nanobots, can self-replicate and quickly get out of control with the risk of substantial damage to the physical world. Self-replication is the modus operandi of genetic engineering, which uses the machinery of the cell to replicate its designs, and it forms the prime danger underlying the "*gray goo*" in nanotechnology, which may destroy life.

Genetics, nanotechnology, and robotics will become so powerful that they may spawn whole new classes of catastrophies and abuses, some of which would be feasible for individuals or small groups of troublemakers to initiate. They would not require large facilities or rare raw materials as was the case with nuclear weapons. Knowledge alone will enable the use of them. Hence, there is the danger of Knowledge-enabled Mass Destruction (KMD), amplified by the power of self-replication.

However, each of these technologies offers untold promise too. The vision of near immortality drives us forward. Genetic engineering may soon provide treatments, if not outright cures, for most diseases. Nanotechnology and nanomedicine can address yet more ills. Together they could significantly extend our average life span and improve the quality of our lives.

If we could agree what we wanted, where we were headed, and why, then by understanding what we can and should relinquish, we would make our future much less dangerous. Otherwise, we can easily imagine an arms race developing over GNR technologies, as it did with the Nuclear, Biological and Chemical (NBC) technologies in the 20th century.

The new Pandora's boxes of GNR are almost open, yet it is hardly noticed. Ideas cannot be put back in a box. Unlike uranium or plutonium, they do not need to be mined and refined, and they can be freely copied. Once they are out, they remain out.

How high are the extinction risks?

The philosopher Leslie (2010) has studied this question and concluded that the risk of human extinction is at least 30 %. Kurzweil believes we have "a better than even chance of making it through", with the caveat that he has always been accused of being an optimist.

Some serious people are suggesting that we simply have to move beyond Earth as quickly as possible. We should colonize the galaxy using von Neumann probes, which hop from star system to star system, replicating as they go. This step will almost certainly be necessary 5 billion years from now or sooner if our solar system is disastrously impacted by the impending collision of our galaxy with the Andromeda galaxy within the next 3 billion years.

Will we survive our technologies?

We are being propelled into this new era with no plan, no control, and no brakes. The breakthrough to wild self-replication in GNR could come suddenly. Building on the relinquishments initiated by the Biological Weapons Convention and the Chemical Weapons Convention, successful abolition of nuclear weapons could help us build a habit of relinquishing dangerous technologies. Verifying relinquishment may be a difficult problem, but not an unsolvable one.

The major task will be to apply this to technologies that are naturally much more commercial than military. There is a vital need for transparency. Verifying compliance will also require adoption of a strong code of ethical conduct resembling the Hippocratic Oath, and having the courage to whistleblow as necessary, even at high personal cost. This requires vigilance and personal responsibility by those who work on both NBC and GNR technologies to avoid enabling weapons of mass destruction and knowledge-enabled mass destruction.

It would seem worthwhile to question whether to take such a high risk of total destruction to gain yet more knowledge and yet more things. There is a limit to our material needs and that certain knowledge is too dangerous and is best forgone. We must find alternative outlets for our creative forces, beyond the culture of perpetual economic growth; this growth has largely been a blessing for several hundred years, but it has not brought happiness, and we must choose whether to continue the pursuit of unrestricted and undirected growth through science and technology with all of the risks that accompany it. Philosopher Thoreau (1817–1862) said that we will be "rich in proportion to the number of things which we can afford to let alone."

The Disappearing Computer

The-computer-as-we-know-it' will have no role in our future everyday lives. It will be replaced by a new generation of technologies. Computing will move off the desktop and ultimately integrate with other objects and everyday environments. Computing will become an inseparable part of our everyday activities, while simultaneously disappearing into the background. It would become a ubiquitous utility, taking on a role similar to electricity, an enabling but invisible and pervasive medium revealing its functionality on request in an unobtrusive way and supporting people's everyday activities.

Reality and Hype

It is the area of strong AI that features more prominently in the public imagination (Arnall 2003). As discussed earlier, the achievement of machine intelligence reaching, or even surpassing our own is deemed as inevitable, perhaps within 30 years. But, in fact, the future of strong AI is highly uncertain, with considerable controversy within the literature concerning whether it is even possible.

Furthermore, the economic and social issues raised by the possibility of strong AI are so fundamental that they cross many academic boundaries, including philosophy, sociology and psychology.

Barriers to Strong AI

The standard test against which the possibility of strong AI is often judged is the Turing Test which discusses the conditions for considering a machine to be intelligent. One famous sceptic of AI is Hubert Dreyfus, who says that a computer will never be intelligent unless it can display a good command of commonsense. This will never be fully grasped because much of our commonsense can only be learned through experience. Thus, since current computers can only really 'represent' things, the possibility of taking a skill, emotion, or something else equally abstract, and changing it into a series of zeros and ones is, according to Dreyfus, close to impossible. A second famous doubter is John Searle, who, with his Chinese Room analogy, has responded directly to Turing. Although a rulebook tells an English–speaking man inside a room how to deal with Chinese sentences which may be perfect Chinese, it does not follow that the man actually understands the language as a native speaker would, rather than merely processing it.

These kinds of convincing rebuttals demonstrate that there are intellectually powerful barriers to the ultimate goal of AI research. Many researchers consider strong AI as neither particularly likely nor even desirable. Although computers are certainly becoming faster, this does not necessarily imply that computers are becoming more intelligent.

Moore's law in hardware development must be contrasted with the fact that computer engineers do not seem to be able to write software much better as computers get more advanced. Even if the ability to program software advances rapidly within the next few decades, it seems likely that the AI laboratories will be incapable of providing the kind of environment necessary for generating well-rounded intelligence. It cannot be expected to build a single, isolated AI alone in a laboratory with much intelligence. This is unless AIs are provided with space in which a rich culture will be evolved with repeated social interaction.

And with things that are like them, you cannot really expect to get beyond a certain stage. Robots lack the dexterity of the human hand, essential for the types of manufacturing that have moved to low-cost locations. *Low-cost dexterous manipulation* is essential if progress is to be made. At present, however, creating dexterous manipulation is beyond researchers. This and similar challenges are unlikely to be met in the next few years. It may be 30–40 years before such technologies are perfected.

A future for strong AI?

In spite of the many fundamental barriers the fields of AI and robotics are replete with many wonderfully inventive predictions, a domain where reality and science fiction often meet. Indeed, it is likely that in the next two decades more and better capabilities will be observed that may be attributed as awareness. However, it is unlikely that machines will ever have human awareness in the philosophical sense of the term, although they may come close in the long term. Rather, we can expect to see classical AI going on to produce more and more sophisticated applications in restricted domains, such as expert systems, chess programs and Internet agents.

Therefore, in conclusion, full AI will not be expected for at least several decades. The reason is that there is no obvious direct path for getting from the simple robots and brittle software programs currently in existence to human-level intelligence. A long series of conceptual breakthroughs are needed, and for this kind of thinking, it is very difficult to anticipate a timetable.

Predictive Intelligence

Artificial Intelligence has a *predictive aspect* which concerns the ability to use software running on powerful computers to analyze information about human behavior. In the private sector, companies are already using predictive intelligence to analyze data profiles and solve more mundane business problems, like marketing to help sellers market more effectively and to identify which customers are more likely to spend the most money.

Another example of this is provided by the US Department of Defense which is mining data sources all over the world to detect, classify and identify foreign terrorists, decipher their plans, and take timely action to pre-empt and defeat their acts. The tools rely to a large extent on new AI technologies. These include "entity extraction" from biologically inspired algorithms for agent control, for face, iris and gait recognition, and for avoiding surprise and predicting future events.

Concerns have emerged in relation to their implications for infringing individual and group privacy, and the possibility of such information being handled carelessly or even leading to malevolence.

Conclusions

Strong AI asks fundamental questions because it necessarily deals with the nature of human–machine relationships. So great are the implications, that the kinds of tools that might be necessary to begin debate over strong AI are not yet available. It is likely that this technology will not occur in the next few decades, although such potentially revolutionary developments should not be downplayed as mere science fiction.

The prospects of these emerging technologies to affect quality of life in the coming decades should be realistically assessed. There can be no decisive conclusions; the industries involved are too dynamic and uncertain to generate any real sense of resolution. Nevertheless, it is possible to highlight a number of important differences and similarities between nanotechnology and AI which go some way to shedding more light on their character.

Perhaps the greatest contrast between the two industries concerns public interest. Nanotechnology is widely regarded as a new and exciting branch of science and technology. This belief has contributed to a massive period of growth in research. AI, on the other hand, is viewed by many as a highly specialized and unproven discipline. The AI community has experienced difficulty in publicizing its own achievements, without provoking general anxiety over machine superiority. This has resulted in a struggle to attract funding in the past, and it is likely that this trend will continue for sometime into the foreseeable future.

Visible similarities also exist between nanotechnology and AI. There has been much talk about the convergence of traditionally separate scientific fields. For example, a confluence of nanoscience, biotechnology, IT, and cognitive science (NBIC) could lead to a tremendous improvement in human abilities, societal outcomes, the nation's productivity and the quality of life. Convergence largely arises from the wide availability of techniques and tools on offer today bringing individuals from traditionally separate disciplines together.

It is possible that developments in nanotechnology could lead to advances in AI through improvements in computer miniaturization, performance, or architecture or through the sensor interface. It may be assumed that any futuristic nanobots would have to be imbued with a reasonable degree of AI.

Any pervasive diffusion of nano- and AI-based technologies in the coming decades will change the structure of the economy greatly. These economic changes will affect politics, the environment, the distribution of income, and our own biology. With the AI revolution, society will undergo perhaps the most radical changes in its history.

References

Acemoglu D, Robinson J (2012) Why nations fail, the origins of power, prosperity and poverty. Crown Business, New York

Agar N (2012) On the irrationality of mind-uploading: a reply to Neil Levy. AI Soc 27:431–436

Almeida e Costa F et al (eds) (2007) Artificial emotions, ECAL, LNAI 4648. Springer, Heidelberg, 223–232

Anderson ML (2003) Embodied cognition: a field guide. Artif Intell 149(1):151–156

Angell M (2011) The epidemic of mental Illness: why? The New York Review of Books

Andreasen NC, Ho B-C, Ziebell S, Pierson R, Magnotta V (2011) Long-term antipsychotic treatment and brain volumes A longitudinal study of first-episode schizophrenia. Arch Gen Psychiatry 68(2):128–137

Arnall AH (2003) Future technologies, today's choices nanotechnology, artificial intelligence and Robotics; a technical, political and institutional map of emerging technologies. Greenpeace Environmental Trust, London

Basu S, Fernald J (2008) Information and communications technology as a general-purpose technology: evidence from U.S industry data. Ger Econ Rev 8(7):146–173

Bedau MA, McCaskill JS, Packard NH, Rasmussen S, Adami C, Green DG, Ikegami T, Kaneko K, Ray TS (2000) Open problems in artificial life. Artif Life 6(4):363–376

Ben-Shahar T (2007) Happier: learn the secrets to daily joy and lasting fulfillment. McGraw-Hill Professional, New York

Block N (1981) Psychologism and behaviourism. Philos Rev 90(1):5–43

Bloom D, Canning D, Sevilla JP (2004a) The effect of health on economic growth. A Prod Funct Approach World Dev 32(1):1–13

Bloom DE, Canning D, Moore M (2004) The effect of improvements in health and longevity on optimal retirement and saving. NBER working paper 10919

Bostrom N (2002) Existential risks. J Evol Technol 9(1)

Breazeal CL (2002) Designing sociable Robots. MIT Press, Cambridge

Brickman D, Campbell J (1971) Hedonic relativism and planning the good society. In: Apley MH (ed) Adaptation level theory: a symposium. Academic Press, New York

Brynjolfsson E, McAfee A (2011) Race against the machine: how the digital revolution is accelerating innovation, driving productivity, and irreversibly transforming employment and the economy. Digital Frontier Press, Sarasota

Buttazzo G (2000) Can a machine ever become self-aware? In: Aurich R, Jacobsen W, Jatho G (eds) Artificial humans, an historical retrospective of the Berlin international film festival 2000. Los Angeles, Goethe Institute, pp 45–49

Buttazzo G (2008) Artificial consciousness: Hazardous questions (and answers). Artif Intell Med 44(2):139–146

Ad J. W. van de Gevel and Charles N. Noussair, *The Nexus Between Artificial Intelligence and Economics*, SpringerBriefs in Economics, DOI: 10.1007/978-3-642-33648-5,

Campbell JY, Lettau M, Malkiel BG, Xu Y (2001) Have individual stocks become more volatile? An empirical exploration of idiosyncratic risk. J Finan 56(1):1–43
Carlip S (2005) Have physical constants changed with time? Physics FAQ
Chalmers DJ (1995) Facing up to the problem of consciousness. J Conscious Stud 2(3):200–219
Chalmers DJ (2010) The singularity: a philosophical analysis, lecture delivered at an event jointly sponsored by Future of Humanity institute of the University of Oxford and the Oxford Centre for Neuroethics
Chrisley R (2003) Embodied artificial intelligence. Artif Intell 149(1):131–150
Cory DG, Fahmy AF, Havel TF (1997) Ensemble quantum computing by nuclear magnetic resonance spectroscopy. Proc Nat Acad Sci USA 94(5):1634–1639
Cowan T (2011) The great stagnation: how America ate all the low-hanging fruit of modern history, got sick, and will (Eventually) feel better. Dutton Publishers, Boston
Csikszentmihalyi M (1990) Flow: the psychology of optimal experience. Harper and Row, New York
Damasio A (1994) Descartes' error: emotion, reason, and the human brain. Avon Books, New York
Dario B (2012) "Avatar" project aims for human immortality by 2045, Gizmag. http://www.gizmag.com/avatar-project-2045/2354/. Accessed 25 Jul 2012
Darwin C (1859) On the origin of species by means of natural selection, or the preservation of favoured races in the struggle for life. John Murray Publishers, London, UK
Dautenhahn K (2007) Socially intelligent robots: dimensions of human—Robot interaction. Philos Trans R Soc B Biol Sci 362(1480):679–704
Davidson D (1987) Knowing one's own mind. In: Proceedings and addresses of the American philosophical association, vol 60(3). pp 441–458
De Grey A (2008) The singularity and the Methuselarity: similarities and differences. In: Bushko RJ (ed) Strategy for the future. IOS press, Dublin
De Landa M (1991) War in the age of intelligent machines. Zone Books, New York
De Long JB (1998) Estimates of world GDP, one million B.C. Present working paper, University of California-Berkeley, California
Dennett D (2005) Sweet dreams: philosophical obstacles to a science of consciousness. MIT Press, New York
Dennett D, Hofstadter D (1981) The mind's I, Fantasies and reflections on self and soul. Bantam Books, New York
Diener E (1984) Subjective well-being. Psychol Bull 95(3):542–575
Diener E, Larsen RJ, Levine S, Emmons RA (1985) Intensity and frequency: the underlying dimensions of positive and negative affect. J Pers Soc Psychol 48(5):1253–1265
Diener E, Seligman MEP (2004) Beyond money, toward an economy of well-being. Psychol Sci Public Interest 5(1):1–31
Di Paolo EA, Rohde M, De Jaegher H (2007) Horizons for the enactive mind: values, social interaction, and play. Cognitive science research papers, University of Sussex, CSRP 587
Dreyfus H (1992) What computers still can't do: a critique of artificial reason. MIT Press, Cambridge
Dunbar RIM (2003) The social brain: mind. Language, and Society in Evolutionary Perspective. Annu Rev Anthropology 32:163–181
Easterlin R (1974) Does economic growth improve the human lot? In: David PA, Reder MW (eds) Nations and households in economic growth: essays in honor of Moses Abramovitz. Academic Press, New York
Evans D (2001) Can Robots have emotions? Chapter 5 in emotion: the science of sentiment. Oxford University Press, Oxford
Ferrucci D et al (2010) Building Watson: an overview of the deep QA project. AI Magazine, Fall issue
Friedman D (2011) The economics of artificial intelligence. http://vimeo.com/9217432
(2011) Futurology, the new overlords; the economist, 10 March 2011
Georgiev D (2004a) Chalmers' principle of organizational invariance makes consciousness fundamental but meaningless spectator of its own drama. Philsci-archive.pitt.edu.eprint 1702

Georgiev D (2004b) Consciousness operates beyond the timescale for discerning time intervals: implications for Q-mind theories and analysis of quantum decoherence in brain. Neuroquantology 2(2):122–145

Gilbert D (2007) Stumbling on happiness. Random House, New York

Goertzel B (2007) Human-level artificial intelligence and the possibility of a technological singularity. A reaction to Ray Kurzweil's The Singularity Is Near and McDermott's critique of Kurzweil. Artif Intell 171(18):1161–1173

Goertzel B, Pennachin C (2007) The Novamente artificial intelligence engine, cognitive technologies. http://wp.novamente.net

Haidt Jonathan (2006) The happiness hypothesis: finding modern truth in ancient wisdom. Basic Books, New York

Hameroff S (1998a) Anesthesia, consciousness and hydrophobic pockets—a unitary quantum hypothesis of anestheticaction. Toxicol Lett 100:31–39

Hameroff S (1998b) Quantum computation in brain microtubules? The Penrose-Hameroff "Orch OR" model of consciousness. Philos Trans Royal Soc Lond A 356:1869–1896

Hamermesh DS, Abrevaya J (2011) Beauty is the promise of happiness? IZA Discussion Paper No. 5600

Hanson R (2008) Economics of the singularity. IEEE Spectrum 4(56):45–50

Hanson R (2009) The economics of brain emulations. In: Healey P, Rayner S (eds) Unnatural Selection: The Challenges of Engineering Tomorrow's People. Earthscan Publishers, London, UK.

Hibbard B (2002) Super-intelligent machines. Springer, Heidelberg

Hurwicz L (1973) The design of mechanisms for resource allocations. Am Econ Rev 63(2):1–30

Jones BF (2009) The Burden of knowledge and the "Death of the Renaissance Man": Is Innovation getting harder? Rev Econ Stud 76(1):283–317

Jones BF (2010) Age and great invention. Rev Econ Stat 92(1):1–14

Judd KL (2006) Computationally intensive analyses in economics, Chapter 17. In: Tesfatsion L, Judd KL (eds) The handbook of computational economics, vol II. North Holland Publishers, Amsterdam

Kahneman D, Diener E, Schwarz N (1999) Well being: the foundations of hedonic psychology. The Russell Sage Foundation, New York

Kasser T, Ryan RM (1993) A dark side of the American dream: correlates of financial success as a central life aspiration. J Pers Soc Psychol 65(2):410–422

Kleinginna PR, Kleinginna AM (1981) A categorized list of emotion definitions, with suggestions for a consensual definition. Motiv Emot 5(4):345–379

Kirsch I (2010) The emperor's new drugs: exploding the antidepressant Myth. Basic Books, New York

Kirsch I, Deacon BJ, Huedo-Medina TB, Scoboria A, Moore TJ, Johnson BT (2008) Initial severity and antidepressant benefits: a meta-analysis of data submitted to the Food and Drug Administration. PLOS Med 5(2):e45

Koch C, Hepp K (2006) Quantum mechanics in the brain. Nature 440:611

Kotlikoff LJ (1979) Some economic implications of life span extension. NBER working paper 155

Kuhn TS (1962) The structure of scientific revolutions, 3rd edn., 1996. University of Chicago Press, Chicago

Kurzweil R (2005) The singularity is near, when humans transcend biology. Viking Press, New York

Langton C (ed) (1995) Artificial life: an overview. MIT Press, Boston

Layard R (1980) Human satisfactions and public policy. Econ J 90(360):737–790

Lederman L (1991) Science—the end of the Frontier. American Association for the Advancement of Science, Washington

Leslie J (2010) The risk that humans will soon be extinct. Philosophy 85(4):447–463

Levine J (1983) Materialism and Qualia: the explanatory gap. Pac Philos Q 64:354–361

Litt A, Eliasmith C, Kroon FW, Weinstein S, Thagard P (2006) Is the brain a quantum computer? Cogn Sci 30(3):593–603

Lucas R (1993) Making a miracle. Econometrica 61(2):251–272
Lykken D, Tellegen A (1996) Happiness is a stochastic phenomenon. Psychol Sci 7(3):186–189
Maddison A (2008) The west and the rest in the world economy: 1000–2030 Maddisonian and Malthusian interpretations. World Econ 9(4):75–100
McDermott D (2006) Kurzweil's argument for the success of AI. Artif Intell 170(18):1227–1233
McGee K (2005) Enactive cognitive science. Part 1: Background and research themes. Constructivist Found 1(1):19–34
McGee K (2006) Enactive cognitive science. Part 2: Methods, insights, and potential. Constructivist Found 1(2):73–82
Maturana HR, Varela FJ (1987) The tree of knowledge: the biological roots of human understanding. Shambhala Publications, Boston
Mauboussin MJ, Schay A (2000) Innovation and markets, how innovation affects the investing process, credit Suisse first Boston corporation report, December 12
Michaud F, Prijanian P, Audet J, L′etourneau D (2000) Artificial emotion and social robotics. In: Parker LE, Bekey K, Barhen J (eds) Distributed autonomous and Robotic systems. Springer, Heidelberg
Minsky M (1988) The society of mind. Simon and Schuster, New York
Minsky M (2006) The emotion machine: commonsense thinking, artificial intelligence, and the future of the human mind. Simon and Schuster, New York
Moravec H (1988) Mind children. Harvard University Press, Boston
Murphy KM, Topel RH (2006) The value of health and longevity. J Political Econ 114(5):871–904
Myers D (2007) Psychology of happiness. Scholarpedia 2(8):3149
Nagel T (1974) What is it like to be a bat? Philos Rev 83(4):435–450
Newell A, Shaw JG, Simon HA (1963) The process of creative thinking. In: Gruber HE, Terrell G, Wertheimer M (eds) Contemporary approaches to creative thinking. Atherton Publishers, New York, pp 63–119
Nordhaus WD (1997) Traditional productivity estimates are asleep at the (Technological) switch. Econ J 107(444):1548–1559
Ozimek A (2012) The rise of the artificial-intelligence economy. The Atlantic
Parker G (2009) Antidepressants on trial: How valid is the evidence? Br J Psychiatry 194(23):1–3
Penrose R (1994) Shadows of the mind. Oxford University Press, Oxford
Penrose R (1997) Physics and the mind. In: Longair M (ed) The large, the small and the human mind. Cambridge University Press, Cambridge, pp 93–143
Pfeifer R, Iida F (2004) Embodied artificial intelligence: trends and challenges. Springer, Heidelberg
Pfeifer R, Scheier C (2001) Understanding intelligence. MIT Press, Boston
Pinker S (2007) The language instinct. Harper Perennial Modern Classics, New York
Reisenzein R (2006) University of Greifswald contribution to the symposium "Agent Construction and Emotions". In: Proceedings of (ACE2006) at the 18th European meeting on cybernetics and systems research, Vienna
Romer PM (1994) The origins of Endogenous growth. J Econ Perspect 8(1):3–22
Sagan C http://en.wikiquote.org/wiki/Carl_Sagan
Sandberg A, Bostrom N (2008) Whole brain emulation: a roadmap, future of Humanity Institute, Oxford University. Technical Report No.3
Scheffer M (2009) Critical transitions in nature and society. Princeton University Press, Princeton
Searle J (1980) Minds, brains and programs. Behav Brain Sci 3:417–424
Seligman MEP (2002) Authentic happiness: using the new positive psychology to realize your potential for lasting fulfillment. Free Press, New York
Seligman MEP (2011) Flourish: a visionary new understanding of happiness and well-being. Free Press, New York
Spinola de Freitas J, Queiroz J (2007) Artificial emotions: are we ready for them? ECAL Stanford Encyclopedia of Philosophy (2003), The Turing Test, http://plato.stanford.edu/entries/turing-test

Stiber M, Holderman T (2004) Global behavior of neural error correction. Paper presented at international, joint conference on neural networks, budapest, hungary
Tesfatsion L (2001) Introduction to the special issue on agent-based computational economics. J Econ Dyn Control 25(3–4):281–293
Tesfatsion L (2002) Agent-based computational economics: growing economies from the Bottom Up. ISU economics working paper No. 115, Iowa State University
Tesfatsion L (2003) Agent-based computational economics: modeling economies as complex adaptive systems. Inf Sci 149(4):262–268
Tesfatsion L (2006) Agent-based computational economics: a constructive approach to economic theory, handbook of computational economics, vol 2. Noth Holland Publishers, Amsterdam, pp 831–880
Thompson E (2007) Mind in life: biology, phenomenology, and the sciences of mind. Harvard University Press, Cambridge
Thompson E, Stapleton M (2008) Making sense of sense-making: Reflections on enactive and extended mind theories. Topoi 28(1):23–30
Torrance S (2005) In search of the enactive: introduction to special issue on enactive experience. Phenomenol Cogn Sci 4(4):357–368
Thoreau HD (1854) Walden: of Life in the Woods. Tickner and Fields Publishers, Boston, MA, USA
Tukey J (1962) The Future of Data Analysis. Ann Math Stat 33(1):1–67
Turing AM (1950) Computing machinery and intelligence. Mind 59:433–460
Vandersypen LMK, Steffen M, Breyta G, Yannoni CS, Sherwood MH, Chuang IL (2001) Experimental realization of Shor's quantum factoring algorithm using nuclear magnetic resonance. Nature 414(6886):883–887
Varela F, Thompson E, Rosch E (1991) The embodied mind: cognitive science and human experience. MIT Press, Boston
Ventura R, Custódio L, Pinto-Ferreira C (2001) Artificial emotions good bye Mr. Spock! FLAIRS—01 Proceedings. AAAI, 150–154
Webb J (2003) Are the laws of nature changing with time? Phys World 16(4):33–38
Weizenbaum Joseph (1976) Computer power and human reason: from judgment to calculation. W. H. Freeman publishers, San Francisco
Whitaker R (2010a) Anatomy of an epidemic: magic bullets, psychiatric drugs and the astonishing rise of mental illness in America. Crown Publishing Group, New York
Whitaker R (2010b) Mad in America: bad science, bad medicine, and the enduring mistreatment of the mentally Ill. Basic Books, New York
Williamson, Oliver E (1998) Transaction Cost Economies, How It Works, Where It Is Headed; De Economist, Vol. 146, No.1, pp. 23–58
Wilson M (2002) Six views of embodied cognition. Psychon Bull Rev 9:625–636
Yudkowsky E (2004) Coherent extrapolated volition. The Singularity Institute, San Francisco
Yudkowsky E (2008) Artificial intelligence as a positive and negative factor in global risk. In: Bostrom Nick, Cirkovic Milan (eds) Global catastrophic risks. Oxford University Press, Oxford
van der Zant CM (2010) Generative AI: a neo-cybernetic analysis. Dissertation, University of Groningen

MIX
Papier aus verantwortungsvollen Quellen
Paper from responsible sources
FSC® C105338

If you have any concerns about our products,
you can contact us on
ProductSafety@springernature.com

In case Publisher is established outside the EU,
the EU authorized representative is:
Springer Nature Customer Service Center GmbH
Europaplatz 3, 69115 Heidelberg, Germany

Printed by Libri Plureos GmbH
in Hamburg, Germany